FUTURE
TRAINING

A Roadmap
for Restructuring
the Training Function

ADDVANTAGE

Improving Human Performance in the Workplace SM

AddVantage Learning Press
A Division of AddVantage Learning, Inc.
Dallas, Texas

Substantial discounts on bulk quantities of *Future Training: A Roadmap for Restructuring the Training Function* are available to corporations, professional associations, and other organizations. For details and discount information, contact the customer services department at AddVantage Learning Press, P. O. Box 702194, Dallas, TX 75370-2194. (800) 458-8844

FUTURE TRAINING

A Roadmap
for Restructuring
the Training Function

James S. Pepitone

Foreword by
Robert M. Canady, Ph.D.
Graduate School of Business and Management
Pepperdine University

FUTURE TRAINING
A Roadmap for Restructuring the Training Function

Library of Congress Cataloging-in-Publication Data

Pepitone, James S., 1947-
    Future training: a roadmap for restructuring the
training function / James S. Pepitone. — 1st ed.
        p.   cm.
    Includes bibliographical references.
    ISBN 0-9635822-1-6
    1. Training. 2. Organizational Effectiveness. 3. Personnel
Management. 4. Organizational Change. 5. Labor Productivity.
6. Business Competition. I. Title

                                            95-75188
                                               CIP

Cover design by David Hutchens, Atlanta, Georgia

Printed in the United States of America

FIRST EDITION
10 9 8 7 6 5 4 3 2 1

ও

I dedicate this book to my clients.
They stand apart in their drive to optimize firm performance;
they understand the powerful synergy of financial,
technical and human factors of operation;
they exhibit a courageous spirit to champion
innovative management practices; and
they achieve exceptional results for all the right reasons.
My brush with death while finishing this book
has given me occasion to recall how indebted I am
to them for their confidence and support —
providing me the opportunity to learn together with them
how to improve human performance at work.

Foreword

by Robert M. Canady, Ph.D.
Interim Dean and Academic Dean
Graduate School of Business and Management
Pepperdine University

Developing and sustaining competitive advantage may well be the last remaining way for an enterprise to distinguish itself from its competitors and thus survive and succeed in today's global economy. Jim Pepitone's *Future Training* focuses on perhaps one of the best but perhaps most overlooked way of achieving this goal: improving human performance and productivity in the workplace. Jim has clearly and convincingly explored this timely subject and offers concrete solutions for companies, executives, managers, and training practitioners.

Corporate managers are missing a significant opportunity, Jim argues, if they have not targeted the performance of their organizations as a means of creating and sustaining competitive advantage. Particularly important for today's companies is their ability to learn and change—abandoning theories and practices that no longer work and embracing concepts and ways of operating that improve human performance in their organizations.

To be truly competitive, companies must maximize the contribution of the corporate training function. But to be a viable player in the process, corporate training must "reinvent" itself, shedding its out-of-date focus, content, and methods. Carefully and thoroughly, Jim provides a road map detailing how the corporate training function can capitalize on its strength—the unique capabilities of its training professionals — to provide the services needed for companies to optimize their capabilities and improve their productivity and performance.

Pepperdine University has played a significant role in the development of the change strategies Jim has articulated so well. As the Interim Dean and the Academic Dean of the Graduate School of Business and Management, I appreciate the recognition that the university has received as a pioneering leader in the field of strategic management of organizational change. Moreover, the instructional methods of the Graduate School of Business and Management are particularly well suited to the adult practitioners, the seasoned managers and executives who know the ropes — and the challenges — of today's corporate institutions.

This book is perhaps not a quick read, but it is a "must read." Having reread the book myself, I have realized a greater depth of understanding each time. Jim has a gift for the integration of concepts others consider abstract, and the vision and courage to confront conventional wisdom — as it needs to be if our organizations are to compete successfully in a global economy. He has set the standard for understanding how enterprises can best invest in and realize the full benefit of their human capital. For this important field, he is the instrument of change.

Culver City, California   Robert M. Canady, Ph.D.

Contents

Acknowledgments

Future Training would not have been possible without the contributions of many clients and colleagues, whose insights and experiences during the past 17 years have proved invaluable in shaping the concepts and prescriptions offered in this work. Writing this book has given me the enjoyable opportunity to revisit my experiences with them, and has proven to me again that it is only through the challenge of application and teaching that we ever fully learn, understand and appreciate knowledge.

To Sue Coffman, my editor, goes my appreciation for her expertise and collaborative spirit and a debt of thanks for her suggestions, advice and relentless revisions.

I also thank Cindy Jacobi for her administrative support — her loyalty, dependability and professionalism have allowed me to meet the day-to-day requirements of a growing business while carving out time to write this book.

To Byron and Marolynn Pepitone, my parents, I take this opportunity to thank them deeply for the sacrifices they made so willingly to see that I received a college education and developed a thirst for knowledge and possibilities. My father's intelligence and mother's love for family have been invaluable gifts.

Most of all, I am grateful for the patience, support, and encouragement of my wife Susie, without whom this book could not have been completed.

All of them deserve credit for what is right about this book. Any errors, omissions or mistakes are mine alone.

About the Author

Jim Pepitone is a principal of Pepitone Berkshire Piaget, management consultants in operations and organization development, and he directs the firm's U.S. and Performance Development practices. Founded in 1978, the firm is recognized by clients worldwide as a leader in performance improvement and problem-solving. Working with executives in some of the world's leading companies, Pepitone Berkshire Piaget consultants have distinguished themselves by their reputation for "*generating competitive advantage for organizations.*" The firm's work has frequently led clients to significant performance differentiation, thus establishing a satisfactory turnaround, sustained market position or subsequent market leadership.

Jim's professional work includes a specialization in the technologies of instruction and human-performance improvement. His creation of Humaneering—a framework to integrate and clarify complex knowledge—has facilitated its transfer to and use by a growing number of organization executives, managers, staff specialists and members. Jim's methodologies for Training Redesign and Internal Consulting for Performance Improvement is used to increase Training's performance impact and cost-effectiveness. Jim's work with Human Resources, Training/Human Resource Development and Organization Development specialists in major organizations has contributed to the realization of new vision for the corporate Training function and to the redeployment of these resources for much greater impact and value-added for their organizations.

Since the early 1980s, Jim has supported the redesign of hundreds of large-scale training programs for a wide array of applications;

as a result, he is now regarded as the "pioneer" in the redesign of training for performance improvement, speed and low cost. Since the early 1990s, his involvement in the field of corporate Training has included the support of numerous clients in the transformation of Training into a greater, more value-adding role in their organizations. He is often sought after for his leadership in redirecting the focus and practices of Training/HRD in large organizations.

Additionally, Jim is an adjunct faculty member of the Graduate School of Business at Southern Methodist University and a certified instructor for the Supplier Training Consortium formed by Motorola, Semetech, Texas Instruments and Xerox. He is a recent vice chair of the Center for Applications of Psychological Type, a not-for-profit research and application-development organization founded by Isabel Myers, co-author of the Myers-Briggs Type Indicator® (MBTI®).

Jim has been CEO of a regional management consulting firm, VP of sales for Automation Industries (NYSE), and general manager for Cybertek (NASDAQ). He earned a B.B.A. in Industrial Management and an M.B.A. from The University of Texas in Austin, and an M.S. in Organization Development from Pepperdine University.

Jim can be contacted at his Dallas office — (214) 343-3500.

Introduction

Corporate Training — *From Resource to Source of Competitive Advantage*

In larger organizations, management provides for a *Training, Training & Development* or *Training/Human Resource Development (HRD)*[*] section — a training resource — to help managers in equipping organization members with the requisite knowledge, skills and attitudes to perform satisfactorily in their current and probable future roles. The specific responsibility of Training practitioners is to make planned instructional interventions that teach organization members how to do their work.

In recent years, this Training function has come under increasing scrutiny regarding its relevance, effectiveness and value for the investment it represents. Our work with clients to improve operational and organizational performance has given Pepitone Berkshire Piaget (PBP) opportunity to examine management's concerns in depth. Management's evaluation is driven by four factors: (1) competitive pressures that have never been greater; (2) the routine challenge to remain profitable and develop strategic competitive advantage; (3) a growing

---

[*] For ease of reading, I will use the word Training to designate all of these functions. When more specific reference is called for, the more common function name is used. For additional clarity, I will capitalize words like *Training, Human Resources, Organization Development, Information Services*, etc., when referring to a function or department of an organization and to the related trade or occupation. I will use a lower-case first letter when referring to activities or programs. Furthermore, throughout the book I will italicize key words and phrases for emphasis, oftentimes when they are first introduced in the text.

lack of confidence in training activity, the result of its negligible impact and increasing costs and time requirements; and (4) concern about its relationship with the practitioners who provide these services, and in particular their evident arrogance, lack of business acumen, and their disrespect for management. In making this evaluation, management is concluding more and more often that the sizable expense and lost productivity required for training and development activity are not yielding an adequate improvement in performance. A reduction of these costs would free cash for other uses and improve profitability. Further complicating this situation, however, management is coming to recognize that the organization itself may ultimately provide the sole avenue for establishing sustainable competitive advantage, and employee training is sure to play a principal role in realizing this potential.

So management is faced with a dilemma: though the Training function helps to prepare organization members to perform in their current roles and will play a dominant role in establishing organizational competitive advantage, it currently represents a significant investment with too little apparent payback. In response, many executives are deciding to reduce their investment in Training through the outright elimination of the function or department, or by restructuring and downsizing to support only mission-critical training requirements. Others are deciding to continue or expand widespread training and development activity, based on their intuitive belief in human potential and their judgment that the investment in people is worthwhile. Still other executives remain uncertain which is the best course of action. Adding to this challenge is the fact that most executives are not well informed about the technology regarding training, learning, maximizing human performance, and so on—beyond inferences from their own experience. Even today, these subjects receive scant treatment even in the best business schools.

Management can benefit greatly from two pieces of information in deciding the fate of its Training investment. First, management needs an objective appraisal of its Training department's current performance in cost-effectively meeting the organization's obvious training needs. This information needs to be specific for the organization but does not need to be exhaustive. For it to be factual and thus useful, though, such a report requires independent inquiry and analysis. This book cannot be a suitable alternative, yet I can generalize about the effectiveness of many corporate Training functions because PBP routinely performs these assessments.

Second, management needs some idea of the possibilities—a sensible picture of what a Training function *could* contribute *if* its mission did not limit its role to providing the customary instructional classes, to targeting minimum acceptable skill levels, or to concentrating on just the human side of business performance. *What if* management mandated that every classroom training program be shortened by 50 percent, reduced materials cost by 50 percent, and then evaluated for its effectiveness both at the end of class and back at work? *What if* management abolished traditional classroom instruction altogether and required that employees learn work skills on their feet, on the job, or on their own time? *What if* management challenged the Training function to fully tap the technologies of human performance—of which Training practitioners have more of an understanding and appreciation than any other organization unit—to provide much more comprehensive support? *What if* the Training function's mission was broadened to make business-performance improvement the measure of success, to make employee performance development the focus for interventions, to make competitive advantage the objective, and to make management's complete satisfaction the goal? In this book, I explore these possibilities.

Just as management may have some difficulty picturing the Training function as doing little more than holding training classes, so will some Training practitioners. The point remains that the untapped potential for human performance holds great promise for organizations, and the Training function is generally underutilized and at the same time uniquely suited to support management's objective of capitalizing on this potential. To begin to imagine the possibilities, consider several objectives that might belong to a staff function that is aggressively supporting management's goal to improve human performance:

- Provide just-in-time training support that is unquestionably effective, fast, low-cost, and flexible.
- Partner with line managers upon request to resolve employee-performance limitations.
- Garner the full support of organization members to reengineer business operations for significant gains in productivity and performance.
- Facilitate the systematic, continuous improvement of the work routines of organization members.

- Expand the organization's performance capability by fostering an organization-wide renaissance in self-initiated employee learning and development.
- Team up cross-functionally with Information Systems, Facilities, Industrial Engineering and Human Resources' Recruiting, Compensation and Benefits sections, to develop and implement whole-systems productivity improvement initiatives.
- Target large-scale employee-provided customer services routinely performed in a perfunctory way and develop distinguishing improvements that transform these services into a source of competitive advantage.

In *Future Training*, I propose a future for the Training function that fully exploits the application of scientific knowledge — technology related to human behavior, learning, performance and productivity — to improve business performance. I recommend the fundamental restructuring of Training, including rethinking and redefining its purpose, redesigning and reengineering its processes, and repositioning and redeploying its resources within the organization. These changes are necessary if Training is to help management solve performance problems and capitalize on the largely untapped potential to improve the performance and productivity of today's workforce of knowledge and service specialists. And for people to become a competitive advantage for organizations, management will require the skilled support of Human Resources and Training practitioners.

Obviously my recommendations challenge the Training function as we know it. Some practitioners may consider my critique of current training practices inappropriate and an unwelcome challenge to their hard work and accomplishments. This would be unfortunate because, in fact, I am stressing their importance to the success of an organization. Their role is pivotal, and that is why as a unique resource they must substantially change their work so that they become many times more effective.

Future Training offers many insights into the potential for corporate training. In addition, readers will learn about methods for improving the cost-effectiveness of human-performance interventions. Much of this technology has emerged as a direct consequence of PBP's work with clients. One such concept is *Training Redesign*, a systematic process for upgrading existing training programs to assert management's economic criteria of performance, speed and efficiency as the central design parameters. Step by step, this process focuses the training design team on methods to make training better, faster and cheaper. A 50 percent reduction of class time and a 50 percent reduction in costs are extraordinary efficiencies made possible by the underemphasis on these criteria during design. Another method I outline briefly is PBP's *Process Guide to Internal Consulting for Performance Improvement*. It supports a new role for the Training practitioner and stresses an action-research approach to developing performance-improving interventions. I also outline, but in more detail, the *Humaneering* process algorithm—a framework for understanding the integration of technology regarding human behavior, learning, performance and productivity—that depicts six distinct stages involved in maximizing the human resource contribution to an enterprise. Strategic guidance for Training leadership is proposed as a four-phase transformation—"from resource to source of competitive advantage." This transformation has proven itself to be a helpful roadmap for this journey, directing leaders to focus on the opportunities and issues of greater importance in an experience-proven sequence. Also, I discuss an innovative structure for organizing and deploying staff support services. The *Convergence Strategy*, as I will refer to it, entails the restructuring of performance-enhancing staff support functions into one matrixed organization that is deployed as internal project consulting teams—representing all relevant technologies—to make effective process interventions. It has proven to be a superior organizing and operating strategy in numerous situations, eliminating staff work that is myopic and maximizing the potential for performance improvement.

Readers unfamiliar with my work might ask how I am qualified to write a book on the future of corporate training. I should begin my answer by pointing out that I am not a Training practitioner, although I routinely educate and train others and utilize training for myself, my professional staff and my clients. Furthermore, I am not a professional manager, although I have managed as a first-line supervisor, as the director of a staff support function, as a general manager for a public company, and as an entrepreneur and CEO who has made his share of tight payrolls.

My work for the past 17 years has been management consulting—assisting companies in the improvement of their business performance—whether leading an operations or marketing team to solve a specific problem, improving the performance and productivity of a sales force or customer service group, developing performance-producing strategy with senior executives, or working with support staff to improve their impact or efficiency. This work has been diverse—in many industries, in start-ups and turnarounds, in global corporate giants and narrowly focused specialty firms, and in many parts of the world—yet whoever the client and whatever the project, the consistent focus has been real, no-excuses performance improvement. Routinely, my work requires me to generate improvements in business performance, which often leads to the design of interventions to effectively change worker capabilities in support of a performance objective. The effectiveness, speed, cost and flexibility of these interventions, which often include training, are paramount. Consequently, to design these interventions with reliability and precision, I use a differential method of diagnosis, draw from an experience-driven taxonomy of intervention designs, operate with an open and participative style to facilitate change, and sustain a constant search for new theory and technology in high-performance work systems. I have taken the same approach to writing this book.

Beyond my consulting experience, my sources for this book include my formal education and industry assignments, coupled with my curiosity and continuing analysis of the emerging human performance technologies. Furthermore, I have utilized PBP's database on the training operations of diverse organizations, including many of the Fortune 500. This database is the product of numerous research studies conducted during the past several years. And finally, the energy for this project comes from my unabashed personal motive to support people who are trying to improve their performance and the performance of their organizations.

One of my intentions in *Future Training* is to put into relevant perspective many of the theories, concepts and practices used to explain work-related aspects of human behavior, learning, performance and productivity; and to offer managers and practitioners a somewhat more integrative alternative that takes up the full complexity of this subject and provides the reader with a guide for better understanding and for taking appropriate action. And recognizing that there is no one best way to manage all organizations, I have taken a descriptive, as much as a prescriptive, approach in my presentation.

Future Training may not be an easy book to read. The needs it addresses are complex, and much greater understanding of contributing factors and forces is required of practitioners in the field. To simplify reading, my only suggestion is to first skim the text to become oriented, and then read for comprehension when an application for its contents arises. I have organized the text into four parts, each with several short chapters, to direct the reader quickly to the issues of immediate interest. Part I, *Training Loses Its Way*, provides valuable historical perspective, albeit through the lens of economic analysis, to detail logically the evolution of training, both the intervention method and the staff support function, to the point of its current insufficiency. In Part II, *Paths for Change*, I present two vignettes, which illustrate a range of responses that begin the process of reinventing the Training function to improve human performance. Then, in Part III, *Performance and Productivity*, I introduce the concept of Humaneering to integrate the wealth of scientific knowledge we can access to improve human behavior, learning, performance and productivity, and subsequently to serve as a framework for better understanding the complex series of interventions required for organizations to maximize their benefit from the human component of business performance. Finally, in Part IV, *Training Gets to Work*, I outline an experience-based strategy for transforming the Training function into a source of competitive advantage. Furthermore, I provide a process overview and brief description of several methods that PBP utilizes to approach many of the challenges now faced by the corporate Training function.

Future Training draws broadly from my work with clients, who will remain nameless.   This practice, which I learned from Peter Drucker, preserves the advantages that my clients have paid me to develop for them while also preventing the reader from overgeneralizing the circumstances of individual companies. I believe every situation is somewhat different, and every management team is obliged to fully consider a generalized strategy in light of its organization's unique characteristics.

For some readers, this book will provide sufficient information for action. For others who would like to have more, PBP routinely provides instruction—in both public and in-house workshops—to transfer this technology for client use.

Dallas, Texas   Jim Pepitone

Part I

Training Loses Its Way

A man was looking on the ground for his lost key.
When his neighbor asked him where he lost it,
he pointed to a different place and said, "Over there."
The neighbor replied, "Then, why not look there?"
The man replied, "Because the light is better here."

Nasrettin Hoca

In 1881, Frederick Winslow Taylor (1856-1915), an American engineer, first applied knowledge to the analysis, study and engineering of *work* itself. His concepts were published in 1911 as *The Principles of Scientific Management*. Taylor's approach was to *study* a task, *engineer* it for high productivity, and then *teach* it as a step-by-step process. His goal was to improve the way work was performed so that it required less time and effort, thereby increasing productivity. He called it "working smarter" (Drucker, 1993).

Taylor introduced the practice of formal training in the workplace as a means of providing workers with the requisite knowledge, skills and attitudes to perform more valuable work. He believed that anyone could learn how to do meaningful work, and he convinced business leaders they could *train* unskilled workers to practice a trade or perform a factory operation requiring skill and precision.

Training fulfilled Taylor's goal of reducing the hostility between workers and management by disproving the previously dominant economic theory that work output could be increased only by working harder and working longer hours. Training also enabled industry to draw from an unskilled population to create its workforce, and to improve productivity by improving the way tasks were performed. And as the productivity of workers grew, so did their wages and standard of living.

By the late 1920s, Taylor's methods had fully changed the way work was designed and the way factory workers were selected and prepared for their tasks. Training had gained broad acceptance as the *process for improving human performance at work.*

In the 1930s, when America was trying to survive the Depression, training enabled people to work productively even when given the opportunity to do work they had never done before. In the 1940s, training made it possible for the U.S. to quickly develop defense production capabilities that made a crucial difference in the Allied victory in World War II. And then, following the war, training prepared the nation to resume civilian life, and it supported one of the most dramatic economic expansions the world has witnessed.

Between 1950 and 1990, the focus of workplace training shifted away from its traditional role of teaching people how to improve the performance and productivity of their work. While the practice of management was still in its infancy and little was understood about how to manage for performance and productivity, training activity became the default solution for virtually every problematic issue involving employees. This shift in emphasis led to an exploding workload for Training practitioners and an endless array of management and employee development programs.

Training activity increased to the point that *Training* was established as an institutionalized staff function, commonly linked to the other human-resource-related activities within most large companies. With this more prominent centralized role, Training practitioners were motivated to promote new training activity. At the same time they distanced themselves from any real concerns of the business and their management customers. Increased training justified more staff and bigger budgets—the principal criteria for increased pay, power and prestige in bureaucratic organizations. The impact was to immediately reduce productivity because considerable employee work time was spent in lengthy classroom training activities. Moreover, these sessions rarely, if ever, produced value in the form of improved performance or productivity.

The competitive pressures of a global marketplace, increasingly sophisticated technology, and dramatic changes in the social fabric of America have ushered in new criteria for decision-making about organization activity, staffing, etc. To *add value* to products or services is now in many companies the only acceptable reason for activities, or costs, to exist. For corporate Training, this practice presents a serious challenge. Because Training has shifted much of its focus away from technical skills training that can improve human performance and increase organizational productivity, too little of its activity has a traceable impact that adds value.

Furthermore, many individual Training practitioners have reduced their added value sufficiently that only token support now remains for their work. Based on a survey of middle- and upper-level managers in Fortune 500 companies conducted by PBP in the spring of 1992, there are many substantial reasons why their value has declined:

- *Insufficient business acumen.* Many Training practitioners lack substantial understanding of (a) the operation of a business, (b) the requirements for survival and success and (c) the challenges of management.
- *Insufficient results.* Many Training practitioners fail to provide support that is genuinely helpful to employees and measurably profitable to management.
- *Insufficient expertise.* Many Training practitioners have too little professional knowledge and skills in their field and in related fields to assure the effectiveness of their work.
- *Insufficient commitment to the firm.* Many Training practitioners are highly motivated to support social priorities or other personal agendas. These loyalties increase the challenges of management.
- *Insufficient loyalty to their customers.* Many Training practitioners speak and act with employees in such a way as to portray management as an adversary.

The overall purpose of this book is to show Human Resources and Training directors and practitioners, as well as executives and managers throughout organizations, how to put the organizational value back into training activity — to train for results, to reduce the time and expense of training activity, and to improve performance and increase productivity in the workplace. Training has a crucial role to play in the future of successful organizations; however, the largely ineffective and wasteful approach to training practiced by many organizations now threatens this future.

To establish a context for my recommendations, I discuss in Part I the history of formal workplace training and the circumstances that have put the future of Training in question. Chapter 1, "Teaching

Work," focuses on the evolution of the capitalistic workplace and the praiseworthy origin of formal workplace training from the late 1800s through World War II. Chapter 2, "Workplace Changes," examines dramatic changes in the workplace, in the lives of people, and in management practices from 1945 to 1995, and discusses the role of corporate Training in these changes. Chapter 3, "Function Follows Form," discusses the shift of corporate Training away from task training and the consequence of organizing Training practitioners as a staff support function. Chapter 4, "Caught Without Value," expands on the great challenge that Training now faces.

1

Teaching Work

work (wûrk) n. 1. Physical or mental effort or activity
directed toward the production or accomplishment of something.
2. Employment. 3. The means by which one earns one's livelihood.

Webster's New Riverside
University Dictionary (1988)

People have been performing *work* of some form or another throughout recorded history and before. And whatever the work is—doing tasks, making parts, assembling products or providing services—it has to be *learned*. We are not born with the innate knowledge and behaviors to perform work; we learn them.*

Prior to the eighteenth century, most people were bound to their work, or trades, for life, often through relations of serf to lord, and generally not free to own property or to move about as desired. The kind of work was determined most often by their circumstances at birth, and it was learned through some combination of observing a master and hands-on experience. Workers acquired the necessary knowledge and behavior largely by copying the actions of people who knew what to do, whether learning from a family how to farm or carry out domestic chores, or learning what they did from whoever knew how to make something or provide a service. A person could not learn

---

*Since this is a book about training, I want to caution the reader not to make the mistake of equating learning with training. They are not the same. Briefly stated, to learn is "to gain knowledge, comprehension or mastery through study or experience," and to train is "to coach in or accustom to a mode of behavior of performance; to make proficient with special instruction and practice." Learning is something one does for oneself, whereas training is something one does for others. The principal goal of training is learning, yet training is neither necessary nor sufficient to cause learning to occur.

a certain kind of work unless others were willing to share what they knew and did, and then learning would take several years. To make matters more difficult, some craft workers were less than eager to share their knowledge with outsiders. Most of the commercial tasks that we now classify as *crafts* were referred to as *mysteries* as late as the year 1700. Possessors of these skills were reluctant to share their secrets because they wanted to preserve the economic value their skills provided. As a result, trades often remained within families for many generations. And those who became apprentices were often sworn to secrecy.

Sometime in the early 1700s, craft knowledge was first transformed into *technology*—a system of rules, principles, methods and materials applied to commercial objectives—to guide and regulate the practice of manual arts and skills. The *Encyclopédie*, published in 1751, assembled in an organized form the *knowledge* of most crafts recognized at the time, consequently allowing even non-apprentices to learn them. The aim was not to produce *new knowledge*, but to convert what existed previously only as mystery, artistry, experience and practice into *textbook knowledge*.

Putting technical knowledge into written form expanded the opportunity to transfer this knowledge, ultimately leading to the establishment of the first agricultural and engineering schools in the mid-1700s and the first medical school in the mid-1800s. The function of these schools was to *teach* accepted technology in the form of principles, concepts, procedures and facts that define and guide effective performance. Distinguished from schools whose purpose was to provide education in the liberal arts, these schools were professional schools or trade schools, and their purpose was to *train* people to do a particular kind of work. In these institutions people could gain the equivalent knowledge and skills of apprenticeship, unrestricted by barriers defined at birth, with consistency in performance and at an incomparably accelerated pace. For all practical purposes, these schools mark the emergence of formal *work training*—the intentional *transfer of technology* to people wanting to perform a specific kind of work.

New Freedoms

Social and economic scholars of this time were fascinated with the new prospects made possible by the development of technology and the potential to acquire technical knowledge from books or schools. These remarkable developments literally enabled people to extend their capability at their discretion. Never before had this been so. Still missing, however, were the *freedom* for individuals to choose their work and the *incentive* necessary for them to offset the hardships associated with learning and change. These issues were finally addressed in *The Wealth of Nations*, published in 1776 by the Scottish philosopher and economist Adam Smith (1723-1790). In his widely acclaimed book, Smith explained how *a market system* founded on the basis of *economic freedom* and *competition* would work and how it would ultimately benefit the general public by replacing the inert trade market that had existed for hundreds of years. Smith reasoned that the drive for *self-betterment* would provide the motive force for individuals to improve their earning ability:

> *But man has almost constant occasion for the help of his brethren, and it is in vain for him to expect it from their benevolence only. He will be more likely to prevail if he can interest their self-love in his favour, and shew them that it is for their own advantage to do for him what he requires of them. Whoever offers to another a bargain of any kind, proposes to do this. Give me that which I want and you shall have this which you want, is the meaning of every such offer; and it is in this manner that we obtain from one another the far greater part of those good offices which we stand in need of. It is not from the benevolence of the butcher, the brewer, or the baker that we expect our dinner, but from their regard to their own interest. We address ourselves, not to their humanity but to their self-love, and never talk to them of our own necessities but of their advantages.*

Smith also asserted that advances in production technology would support workers by continuously improving their productivity. These gains would then yield increased wages and an ever-higher standard of living for workers.

The fundamental characteristics of work were re-created during the late 1700s, starting first in England around 1750 and soon spreading through Europe and to the U.S., and precipitating a time of great challenge and dramatic social change for most people. *The Declaration of Independence*, signed on July 4, 1776, called for a completely new society dedicated to "life, liberty, and the pursuit of happiness." *The Wealth of Nations*, published in the same year, provided the plan for the way such a society could operate. At its founding, the U.S. was a unique nation resolutely based on the *capitalist* principles of *economic freedom* — *individual freedom, private property* and *free-market trading* — that called for an extraordinary amount of individual *self-responsibility* from its citizens. Unlike people in pre-existing societies in Europe and Asia, Americans were not bound to a trade for life, and they were able to contract or withhold their labor and to own property.

For many people, *intellectual and economic emancipation* was a precious achievement—the very reason for founding the U.S. Yet because these concepts were instituted by scholars and power holders, emancipation was unwelcome progress for many others. Most people affected had little control over the ensuing changes to the characteristics of work and society, and accordingly were involuntarily separated from their traditions and faced an uncertain future. Along with the opportunity and fulfillment possible with economic freedom came the inherent unrest, insecurity and potential suffering associated with accepting responsibility for oneself, plus the hardships associated with fundamental *change* of this enormity. Many people escaped indentured status only to find working for a wage a more uncertain existence. Others found their traditional craft no longer wanted, suddenly replaced by a machine-made alternate. For all, the time-honored ways of living and working were giving way to machines, factories and employment. As a result, antagonism ran high between the common people who sensed the destruction of their world and the industrialists who saw this change as welcomed progress. As consultant and author William Bridges concludes in *JobShift*, "In these reactions, we can see the beginning of a great divide in modern thinking between those who follow the line of socioeconomic development and those who take a more humanistic path"(1994). From history, though, we know this division was not new, only reframed. Those who preferred economic freedom and seized its opportunities were just replacing the totalitarian aristocracy as the illusory enemy of the common people.

Between 1780 and 1880—the period in which the *Industrial Revolution* took place—new technology-driven products and improved labor productivity, coupled with the exercise of economic freedom, led the U.S. through an unprecedented economic expansion. Trades developed into industries, and craft work was replaced with machine labor. The development of machine technology fueled the concentration of production into large-scale *factories*, which required large amounts of capital, energy and human labor to operate. With the advent of technology, it became possible to teach a particular task or type of work to people who wanted to learn, thus enabling companies to prepare a workforce of the size required for *mass production*. Previously landless laborers and immigrants with newly acquired political and economic freedoms rushed to factory jobs, which promised an escape from poverty and desperation.

The transformation from an *agrarian* to an *industrial* economy ultimately established *employment* as a new paradigm of the way most people earned their livelihood. People were anxious to have the benefits companies offered, which often included lodging, board, and education as well as a decent wage and training to enable them to perform the work. In 1780, approximately 80 percent of the population was *self-employed,* and the remaining 20 percent worked for companies as *wage and salary employees.* By 1880, only 37 percent of the population remained self-employed (M. Reich, 1978).

Thus it was large-scale mass production, born of technology and fueled by economic freedom for all, that provided a new *economic opportunity* for Americans regardless of their heritage. For most people, it provided the first chance to choose their work and thereby gain new discretionary power in regard to earning a living.

New Challenges

This period of developing technology and emerging economic freedom was a time of extraordinary social change, unrest and personal anguish for many people. One perception of the Industrial Revolution sees the extraordinary disruption to time-honored routines—the very painful introduction of an economic way of life based on machine technology and economic principles utterly alien to lifestyles existing for hundreds of years beforehand. Furthermore, neither business owners nor workers had much experience in operating large companies effectively or in functioning in the new employment relationship, and discord naturally ensued. No one really understood how to deal with the many new problems consequent to a large workforce, modern technology, dangerous machinery and large-scale operations. A good example is the persistent worker resentment of the oppressive treatment by supervisors, when in fact supervisors were simply practicing the methods of supervision known at the time. As craftspeople, workers had been free to do as they pleased when they pleased. Not so as employees. Now subject to the *command and control* of supervisors, workers resented their now-limited discretion.

The many challenges and widely felt hardships accompanying the emergence of a market economy, both in Europe and the U.S., led to growing antagonism between workers and owners in the nineteenth century. Karl Marx (1818-1883), a German philosopher, socialist and staunch critic of capitalism, wrote of the inherent "instability" of capitalism, its "uncertainty" and "wavering growth" due for the most part to the opposing demands of "labor and capital," and the fact that neither had ultimate "control over the other." These views paint a more precise portrait of the market economy at work, whereas Adam Smith's vision was written in more theoretical terms.

Although the loyalties of both Marx and Smith lay with workers rather than with owners, these two great minds clearly disagreed as to how workers would fare in a market economy. Marx, along with most other nineteenth-century economists and prominent engineers, was convinced that work output could be increased only by making workers work *harder* or work *longer hours*. Ironically, Marx's argument was sufficiently convincing that for a time unenlightened owners were motivated to increase worker output precisely in this way—by stressing longer hours and greater hardship for workers—the very same conditions Marx predicted in hopes of preventing. Smith had argued that advances in technology would lead to improvements in worker productivity, which would result in increased wages and living standards for workers.

Organizing and Managing Work

Machines reflected the great achievement of society at the turn of the twentieth century and ultimately became the metaphor for organizing and managing work. In comparison to agrarian ways of working, machines increased human productive ability many thousand times. The pursuit of these machine-based increases in capability, however, soon influenced virtually every aspect of people's lives. People made adjustments to their established routines in order to live and work around the time schedule and particular needs of machines: people became the flexible resource, adjusting to the inherent inflexibility of huge production machinery.

It is not hard to imagine, then, that the organization and management of work at the turn of the century would also follow the design of machines. Organizations were not established as ends in themselves. . . . they were instruments created to make this new machinery productive. In fact, the word *organization* is derived from the Greek work *organon*, meaning "a tool or instrument." In other words, history has consistently portrayed organizations as mechanical devices developed to perform some kind of productive function. Therefore, it is understandable that organizations have been oriented around tasks, objectives, skills, plans and goals, and that members have been expected to behave as if they were parts of machines — routinized, efficient, reliable and predictable.

Specific rules for organizing and managing work evolved from concepts pioneered by Frederick the Great of Prussia, who ruled from 1740 to 1786. Frederick inherited an unruly mob for an army and set out to apply practices of Roman armies and of European armies of the sixteenth century, combined with his own concepts inspired by the mechanical inventions of his day. He set out to shape his army into a reliable and efficient instrument, introducing such concepts as ranks, uniforms, regulations, task specialization, standardization of equipment, command language and systematic training. The concepts that mechanized Frederick's army were gradually transferred to factories of this era (Morgan, 1986).

Adam Smith's vision for a market economy was based heavily on specialization and the division of labor. In 1801, Eli Whitney, an American inventor, first demonstrated the potential for mass production with his public demonstration of how guns could be assembled from piles of interchangeable parts. Many other insights and applications of these principles followed. However, it was not until the early twentieth century that these concepts were synthesized into a comprehensive theory of organization and management.

Henri Fayol (1841-1925), a Frenchman, was one of the more prolific writers among the early management theorists in the U.S. and Europe in the early twentieth century. These theorists were interested in the practical problems of management and sought to assemble the current knowledge about organizations. Drawing from military and engineering principles that were applied in successful organizations, they set the basis for many current management techniques. Fayol's *"fourteen management principles,"* represented in **Figure 1.1**, summarize many of the general principles of classical management theory for organizing and managing work.

Training to Improve Performance and Productivity

Frederick Taylor stood alone among factory foremen in his concern for the average worker, and was particularly distressed at the demonstrated lack of compassion and support for workers shown by factory

Figure 1.1
Fayol's "Fourteen Management Principles"

Principle	Description
1. Division of Labor	To increase efficiency, workers should specialize in tasks for which they are best suited.
2. Authority	Managers should have authority, the right to issue orders. With authority comes responsibility for ensuring that the work is done.
3. Discipline	The organization should expect obedience from its employees, and in turn, employees should expect to be treated with dignity by their employers.
4. Unity of Command	Each employee should report to only one supervisor.
5. Unity of Direction	Each activity of an organization should have one leader and one plan.
6. Subordination of Personal Interests	Management must ensure that decisions are made from a rational standpoint and not solely to placate self-interested individuals or groups.
7. Remuneration	People should be paid in order to motivate them.
8. Centralization	The issuing of orders creates a degree of centralization in all organizations. However, it is possible to increase employee autonomy (decentralization) or decrease it (centralization).
9. The Scalar Chain	Authority is hierarchical and must be made explicit. In other words, it must be clear who reports to whom.
10. Order	All materials and all activities should be kept where they are appropriate.
11. Equity	Employees should be treated justly.
12. Stability of Tenure	People resources should be planned for.
13. Initiative	Managers should encourage workers to be enthusiastic about their work.
14. Esprit de Corps	Management should encourage harmony and discourage destructive conflict within the organization.

(Rothwell and Stredl, 1992)

foremen. Taylor's concern ultimately prompted his study in the early 1880s of *work design*—how factory tasks were designed and accomplished—as a viable approach for improving relations between the two groups. His goal was to reduce the hostility between workers and owners by making workers more productive through the redesign of their work, which in turn would increase their value to owners and thus justify better wages and increased respect (Weisbord, 1987).

Before Taylor's studies, intelligent people felt it was beneath them to apply their knowledge to work. Labor was labor, and they wanted little part of it. Taylor, however, took a job in a foundry after his poor eyesight prevented him from entering Harvard. His exceptional capabilities soon elevated him to foreman. From this perspective Taylor learned the real hatred of the workers for their employers, and he began to study work to determine how it could be better accomplished (Drucker, 1993).

Taylor's approach was to study tasks and design ways to accomplish them most efficiently—with a minimum of worker time and effort. To do this, Taylor would observe workers as they instinctively completed a task, and then collect data on the physical and mental activities involved. Then he would solicit the one or two best workers from the group and strive, with their assistance, to redesign the task, trying to eliminate unnecessary time and motion as well as material waste. Taylor's manner was very self-effacing, so workers were ordinarily quite willing to help him in these redesign efforts. Once the optimum design of the task was determined, the new approach would be taught to all the workers. By tapping into the potential of technology—the best practices for completing a task—Taylor believed he could teach anyone who wanted to learn how to do meaningful work.

Taylor's process of work design—*studying* a task, *engineering* it for high productivity, and then *teaching* it as a step-by-step process—revolutionized the character of physical work. He believed that the secret to high productivity was finding the right challenge for each person, and paying for increased output. Furthermore, he saw management's role as one of *supporting* workers by providing them with whatever tools, equipment, and training they required. Taylor divided the work of supervisors into eight tasks—set-up, machines, quality control, repairs, schedules, specifications, time/cost and discipline—each assigned to a separate foreman, because he thought specialists could be more thorough. Dividing up supervisory authority had the effect of making the foremen "servants of the workmen." Foremen were there to implement a rational system of work, not to boss people

Figure 1.2
Taylor's "Scientific Principles"

Science, not rule of thumb.

Harmony, not discord.

Cooperation, not individualism.

Maximum output, not restricted output.

Development of each man to his greatest

efficiency and prosperity.

– Frederick W. Taylor
The Principles of Scientific Management

---

around. As this management approach demonstrates, Taylor believed that there was "one best way to work." Taylor's views paralleled those of another "early-day humanizer of bureaucratic systems," Mary Parker Follett, who called this premise "the law of the situation" (Weisbord, 1987). In 1915 Taylor finally published his work as *The Principles of Scientific Management*, which was widely acclaimed by business owners and scholars. Taylor's principles ultimately became a foundation for the Harvard Business School and later for Dartmouth's Amos Tuck Business School. (See **Figure 1.2**.)

Based on his work, Taylor could easily be considered the father of *productivity improvement*, the father of *consulting* and the father of *corporate training*. According to Peter Drucker, management professor and historian, Taylor's concepts have sustained an average four percent compounded increase in the productivity of workers making and moving things in the U.S. for more than 100 years. Furthermore, Taylor's fundamental belief that any person willing to learn could be trained to effectively perform any well-designed task opened the doors of the U.S. workplace to the nation's diverse population. In fact, *workplace training* based on Taylor's principles is probably more responsible than any other single development for (a) the unsurpassed economic development of the U.S. in the twentieth century, (b) the rapid expansion of U.S. production capacity and the development of a fighting force capable of winning World War II, and (c) the current high standard of living for factory workers.

"Taylor's greatest impact all told was probably in training," says Drucker. Before Taylor, apprenticeship programs consisted of practical experience gained working under a master for three years, five years, even twenty years in some cases. To prepare for World War II, the U.S. applied Taylor's training approach to create highly skilled technicians in just a few months. Furthermore, Taylor's approach is credited with the rapid development of the Pacific Rim nations following the war. Drucker contends, "Taylor-based training became the one truly effective engine of economic development. The *application of knowledge to work* explosively increased *productivity* [emphasis mine]. Since Taylor began, productivity has increased some fiftyfold in all advanced countries. On this unprecedented expansion rest all the increases in both standard of living and quality of life in the developed countries." Drucker also makes the point that most of this additional productivity has directly benefited workers—a roughly 50 percent increase in purchasing power, a 40 percent decrease in work hours, and improvement in healthcare benefits (Drucker, 1993).

A Reputation for Adding Value

Once understood, Taylor's legacy to the Training field is hard to fault. Then why, you ask, is the "father of corporate training" often spoken of in faultfinding terms within the Human Resources field? There are three probable causes for Taylor's often-maligned reputation. First and most common, most people are simply uninformed, choosing to restate hearsay or rely on myth to form their judgments. Second, Taylor is criticized for the inappropriate application of his concepts, actions which can be the responsibility only of others directly related to the specific situation. Third and most vicious, Taylor's reputation still suffers today because his public image was ruthlessly slandered by the labor unions of his day.

The leaders of skilled-trade monopolies were threatened by Taylor's concept that a person could be trained to do their kind of work. Union leadership wanted work restricted to only their members, and they were successful in securing political support for their position. The unions stimulated a widespread uprising against Taylor and his methods, culminating in Congressional hearings that presented Taylor as the "enemy of the working man."

Further smearing Taylor's public image, the "human relations school" also portrayed Taylor and his methods as the "enemy." Specifically, Taylor was faulted for what neither he nor anyone else understood at the time of his work—that once people's basic security needs were met, they often looked to work for satisfaction of their social and actualization (i.e., non-economic) needs. The slander of Taylor's reputation lingers today, although the facts do not support this negative view.

It is important for Training practitioners and management to understand and appreciate the roots of workplace training and the vital standardization objective for which it was conceived. Taylor's concepts for improving productivity actually tempered the inhumanity of labor practices in the late nineteenth century. They opened the doors of factories and provided a much higher standard of living to workers with no education, trade, skill or relevant prior experience. For most of the immigrants, farm workers and servants who eagerly sought out this well-designed work, it was the first humane job they had had. Factory work was easy to learn because of training. It provided real earning potential, reduced the number of hours that people had to work, and significantly increased the standard of living of those lucky enough to secure positions.

Ultimately, Taylor's organizing and standardizing methods gained wide acceptance in preparing millions to staff large bureaucratic organizations. As a direct result, the U.S. achieved steady increases in industrial productivity and emerged as the leading economic force in the twentieth century. On this reputation, *training* established itself as a *design rule* for achieving high-value work in large organizations.

2

Workplace Changes

By World War II . . . the command and control organization was rapidly growing outdated and was no longer adequate to the needs of the future.

Peter F. Drucker
Post-Capitalist Society (1993)

The U.S. won World War II largely because it was successful in applying a "command and control" organization design to civilian industry. Companies in every major industry were transformed and expanded to produce vast quantities of war-required materials and services.

Immediately following the war, U.S. industry went to work re-converting its wartime capacity, and further expanding it, to focus on the country's neglected infrastructure and to quench the tremendous post-war consumer demand for homes, automobiles, appliances, furniture, and consumables like clothing, food and leisure-time services. Bureaucracy, with its characteristic "command and control" management style, was the existing form of organization structure left over from the war effort, and was well accepted based on the shared military experience of most employees and managers. A dominant concern of most companies at the time, however, was how to best manage the growth and the expanding size of organizations.

Management Revolution

The late 1940s and early 1950s marked a formative period in the development of management thinking; much was still not known about managing larger business organizations which were emerging. *"Management as a discipline only emerged after World War II,"* according to Drucker (1994). In fact, the first major contribution to the formation of a management technology was Drucker's now-famous book, *The Practice of Management,* published in 1954. Initially, management practice was patterned for bureaucratic structures, the dominant paradigm for organizations, but as early as the 1950s it was evident to many that significant change was needed and inevitable. However, it was not until the 1970s that astute management had sufficient insight into new alternatives to recognize the nature and direction of likely changes, and to realize that appropriate management methods would ultimately vary with the circumstances and goals of an organization.

The entire *"Management Revolution"* — Drucker's term for our growing understanding of what management really means — spanned less than 50 years, from 1945 to 1990, and entailed the maturing of our concepts for managing all kinds of organizations, not just businesses. It is telling to note how Drucker's personal definition of management has evolved during this period from *"responsible for the work of subordinates"* during World War II, to *"responsible for the performance of people"* in the early 1950s, to *"responsible for the application and performance of knowledge"* today (1994). Its transition reflects management's natural adaptation to the substantial challenges that it has faced during this period. Those who have been involved with organizations or otherwise in tune with management philosophy and technology as they have developed will recall, and likely with frustration, the seemingly itinerant shifting of priorities every few years, from mass production to organization design, to strategic planning, to finance, to marketing, to quality, and so on, as a changing environment redirected management's development priorities.

Although the bureaucracy's machine-like control and predictability were initially familiar and welcomed by many employees after the war, it was ill-matched to the freedom and affluence most Americans were enjoying in other parts of their lives. Soon people sensed this disconnection or sense of conflict between their work lives and their personal lives. The workplace, many felt, was an alien environment where they were not appreciated as whole persons. Rather, they were treated only as workers, just a part of the machine. A conflict ensued that now seems predictable. Managers, naturally adapting to their responsibility for ever-expanding operations, added more and more structure, policies and procedures to maintain adequate control. Employees, feeling more and more secure, if not invulnerable, became less willing to appreciate, accept or even endure this control. Widespread employee dissatisfaction with management and organization life subsequently surfaced throughout large organizations.

Efforts to apply Taylor's scientific management principles (i.e., division of work, work simplification, and standardization training) to manage and improve the productivity of a growing white-collar workforce met with mixed results. These concepts were successfully applied to design the many new kinds of work that resulted from new products and services and from new support services added to address the internal needs of large organizations. However, the mechanistic principles that had been so successful in increasing productivity in production tasks were for the most part ineffective in increasing white-collar productivity. The increased security, higher standard of living, and educational opportunities that white-collar workers enjoyed led them to *look for more from work* than just getting a paycheck, and to resist narrowly defined jobs and controlling management practices. They sought work that was more in line with their values and self-concept overall — work that provided respect, a voice in decisions and future opportunities. These expectations symbolized new concerns for organizations and new challenges that managers were not equipped or experienced enough to resolve.

Human Relations Training

The search for ways to make work more meaningful, coupled with the social challenges presented by the growing size and complexity of organizations, attracted the influence of psychology as it could be applied to the workplace. This preoccupation led to new research on group behavior, motivation and management methods, as well as new theories and techniques on instruction and behavior change. It also prompted the use of training to teach and support emerging social concepts regarding work and management.

Prominent social psychologists theorized that employees were *de*motivated by their work because of mechanistic job designs, controlling organization structure and insensitive management. Much of this thinking stemmed from the work of George Elton Mayo (1880-1949), an Australian-born psychology professor at Harvard who in the 1920s and 1930s conducted the now infamous research at the Hawthorne Works of Western Electric. In his research, Mayo established what is now commonly referred to as the "hawthorne effect" — that psychological

factors significantly affect worker attitude, motivation and performance. Because this finding challenged Taylor's theories, vicious contro-
versy ensued, creating great division between advocates of Taylor's
"scientific management" and newer disciples of Mayo's "human relations school." Though Mayo's research findings have since been substantially discredited due to evidence of his sloppy research methods,
his conclusions have had a major impact on organization theory and
management practices. Mayo failed to accurately report that work
measurement, pay for performance and frequent feedback figured in
the results, thus reaching the unfounded conclusion that by *just* noticing workers and taking them seriously, management could improve
worker attitude, motivation and performance (Parsons, 1974; Gilbert
and Gilbert, 1994; and Brethower, 1994).

At the time, this diagnosis, whether accurate or not, was
accompanied by too little data to be taken seriously enough by managers to prompt radical changes. Consequently, the problem was not addressed in a substantive way at that time. Management, still
unaccustomed to the growing problem of unmotivated workers, and
unaware of the real solution, ultimately yielded to repeated recommendations for management training in "human relations" skills in
hopes of silencing complaints. Many Training practitioners, driven by
their personal values favoring social over economic concerns, and
frustrated with management's indifference to emerging human concerns, became strong advocates of human relations training. Increased
training activity also meant greater importance and a more imperious
role for trainers, who themselves received only modest respect for their
craft. Following a 10,000-year precedent of training-by-expert, workplace training was reduced to a machine-like process—Instructional
Systems Design (ISD)—which prepared trainers to teach subjects in
which they were not proficient or accomplished (Dick, 1993). Being a
teacher no longer meant one was a master; training was soon known as
the career alternative for those who could not perform.

Though human relations training did not silence the complaints of management, it silenced the reproach of critics demanding
that management do something about steadily worsening worker morale. Management soon recognized training as a tactic for quieting its
faultfinders, unwittingly applying Mayo's assertion—"*just* noticing
workers and taking them seriously"—to contain his own disciples.
Thus the practice of using training as a universal human intervention
was adopted by managers. "Throwing training at the problem" soon
became the solution to a multitude of challenges which management

was not yet capable of solving—problems emanating from a growing and dissatisfied workforce.   As a placebo, training was effective, affordable and seemingly risk-free.   The role of Training practitioners was made permanent as it became clear that a steady volume of training activity lay ahead.   At this point, Training was made a permanent staff support function in larger organizations, its budget and staff challenged only periodically in years of low profitability.   Legitimately viewing training as a *potentially* helpful solution, management did not anticipate the negative consequences that would result.

As one CEO thinks back to describe the situation, "To prescribe training to resolve this complex dilemma, or even to insinuate that one could effectively transform the human relations practices of managers with training programs per se was cause enough to question this diagnosis."   Harvard professor and current Secretary of Labor Robert B. Reich confirms the fallacy of this approach in his best-seller, *The Next American Frontier*:

> *Human-social skills soon became another aspect of professional management, another unit of professional training.   Production workers needed to be made to feel as if they were involved in the enterprise and were respected as individuals.   Actual participation and personal respect were, of course, impractical.   But professional managers could at least manufacture the appearance of involvement and respect* (1984).

Worse yet, this treatment of the problem did not address workers' valid concerns in a substantive way, did not solve industry's productivity problems, and did not pave the way for future improvements. Altogether, the "throw training at the problem" solution did remarkable harm and only trivial good.   It created a further decrease in productivity, as a result of the classes people were required to attend, and wasted virtually all of a sizable investment of resources.   Furthermore, because training often lacked legitimate management support, the disingenuous ambiance surrounding much of the training galvanized an already-festering attitude of cynicism in employees toward management and training, still a prevalent condition in many organizations today.

The goals of programs launched to teach human relations skills and new management practices were not well understood by Training practitioners, not well accepted by management, and not well supported by the predominantly bureaucratic organization culture.

Moreover, it was frequently not clear or convincing to many who were taught just how these concepts would favor workers or existing management or contribute to performance. This lack of confidence in these training initiatives confirmed what savvy Training practitioners have been trying to explain to managers all along — for workplace training to work, it must be needed by management, wanted by the employee, and well-supported by the management systems and culture of the workplace.

Designing a New Workplace

The bureaucratic structure and scientific method of work design represented a tremendous leap forward in the organization and management of work, and facilitated the development of large organizations that would have not been possible with the preceding family-like designs of organizations. Companies and their workers achieved levels of performance and productivity previously unattainable, due largely to optimized individual performance, increases in scale, and improvements in coordination between organizational units. However, this success brought with it serious limitations, including (1) inflexibility and lack of responsiveness during times of uncertainty and change, (2) the inability to capitalize on people's discretionary effort, judgment and creativity, and (3) the failure to satisfy employees' intrinsic desire for worth and accomplishment.

Though the success of the machine-like workplace peaked in the late 1920s, it established a paradigm for industrial organization that persists in the minds of many executives, managers and employees as the "right" way to design and manage productive enterprises . . . well after demonstrating its limitations. Beginning in the 1940s, management theorists and practitioners pioneered several techniques to compensate for the limitations in the current workplace. Despite initial reports of success in many of these innovations — team-building, job enrichment and enlargement, participative management and others — their contributions were always short-lived. These innovations were based on a set of assumptions that were inconsistent with the existing machine-bureaucracy culture that eventually prevailed. To many, it became clear that an entirely new paradigm was needed if organizations were to overcome current limitations.

Kurt Lewin (1890-1947), a social psychologist, is prominent among the many theorists searching for this new paradigm. Lewin

Figure 2.1
Example of Lewin's "Force Field Analysis"

Objective: Improve Teamwork

Status Quo
Line

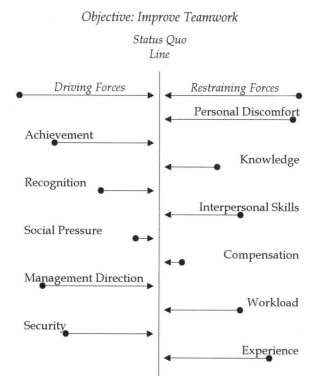

aspired to formulate a set of formal principles that would improve human affairs in the workplace, just as Taylor had 40 years before. Lewin's fascination with the *psychology of work* led to early research regarding the human consequences of farming technology. The title of an essay he wrote in 1920 clearly links this effort to his predecessor: "Humanization of the Taylor System: An Inquiry into the Fundamental Psychology of Work and Vocation." Lewin accepted the conclusion that Taylor's scientific management increased output and cut costs, while simultaneously increasing wages and reducing worker hours and stress. But he knew there had to be more, that work had value beyond pay in giving purpose to human life. Lewin felt that "work should not limit *personal potential* but develop it"(Weisbord, 1987). He suggested that psychologists and efficiency experts should join forces to enhance

Figure 2.2
Comparison of McGregor's Theories "X" and "Y"

Theory "X" Assumptions	*Theory "Y" Assumptions*
1. People have an inherent dislike of work and will avoid it if possible.	1. Work is as natural as play or rest, and will be a source of satisfaction or punishment depending on conditions management can control.
2. Most people must be coerced, controlled, directed and threatened with punishment to achieve organizational objectives.	2. People will exercise self-direction and self-control in achieving objectives to which they are committed.
3. People prefer to be directed, wish to avoid responsibility, have little ambition and want security above all.	3. Commitment comes from rewards that satisfy needs for status, recognition and growth.
	4. People seek and accept responsibility; avoidance is a consequence of experience.
	5. Many people have the creativity and ingenuity to solve organizational problems.
	6. The intellectual potential of people is only partially utilized by modern industry.

both *productivity* and *satisfaction*. This insight filled the gap in Taylor's methods.

Working with Ronald Lippitt, a social scientist, Lewin found striking evidence of the increased potential of democratic management. His contributions to post-industrial management were enormous, but he, like Taylor, is frequently not given due credit by executives or Human Resources practitioners. Consultant Marvin Weisbord, who has conducted considerable research on Lewin's work, emphasizes the scope of his influence:

Lewin's stamp is everywhere in contemporary management: running meetings, work design, team development, systems change, cultural change, leadership styles, participative methods, minority-majority relationships, survey feedback methods, consultation skills (1987).

Lewin's better-known contributions include the following:

- Field theory (See **Figure 2.1.**)
- The change process of unfreezing-moving-refreezing
- Group influence on individual behavior
- Stakeholder participation in change management
- Experience-based learning
- Process consultation

Another prominent theorist, Douglas McGregor (1906-1964), helped Lewin begin the Research Center for Group Dynamics at the Massachusetts Institute of Technology, and later recruited other now-renowned faculty, including Richard Beckhard, Warren Bennis, and Edgar Schein. In fact, McGregor and Beckhard coined the term *organization development* to describe their innovative "bottom-up" change method — starting with the requirements of the external environment and the work to be performed — contrasted with the customary top-down approach. McGregor was one of the first organization consultants to stress the strategic importance of personnel policies regarding

- performance appraisal
- compensation methods
- goal-setting
- labor relations
- values
- culture
- training

McGregor's most noted work, *The Human Side of Enterprise* (1960), and its widely acclaimed yet controversial concept, "Theories X and Y," put into uncomfortably clear management perspective the universal philosophical question of how to treat people. (See **Figure 2.2.**) In McGregor's own words,

> *Once management becomes truly persuaded that it is seriously un-*
> *derestimating the potential represented by its human resources–*
> *once it accepts assumptions about human behavior more consistent*
> *with current social science knowledge than those of Theory X–it*
> *will invest the time, money, and effort not only to develop im-*
> *proved applications of such ideas as have been discussed in these*
> *pages, but to invent more effective ones.*

Although some noteworthy companies embraced McGregor's thinking on participative management and capitalized on its effectiveness at that time, many would wait 20 years for Total Quality Management (TQM) before giving participative management a try. McGregor died in 1964 while he was still writing *The Professional Manager*, which contained the earliest description in management terms of a totally new kind of workplace designed as a "whole system."

Discovering a New Paradigm

Eric Trist (1909-), a social scientist on the faculty at London's Tavistock Institute of Human Relations, and Kenneth Bamforth, a student at Tavistock, uncovered an entirely new way of working during an industrial action research project in 1949. Trist had admired Lewin's work and supported his conclusions that improvements in technology alone, as with scientific management, might increase but would not *maximize* workplace productivity. He also knew from the work of colleagues that attempts to better human relations were ineffective by themselves. Trist and Bamforth then discovered that technology and human relations were, in fact, interdependent, and that productivity was increased significantly by recognizing their integration and by placing work under control of the workers.

In earlier research, Major Wilfred Bion, a psychiatrist, had designed a "leaderless group" method for officer selection that required candidates to *compete* in a test that required *cooperation*. Trist recognized that the reaction of officer candidates closely paralleled the reaction to similar circumstances in a bureaucratic workplace. Employees at all levels are affected by their feelings about authority in ways that end in conflicts, aggression, passivity, demoralization, and withdrawal. As Weisbord has written,

When people fight, run away from the task, pair up defensively, or depend on a leader to solve their problems, they become childish, immature, and unable to grow. They cannot use their creativity or commit to joint action. The constructive course, in a group or a large organization, is to join with others in purposefully defining and carrying out mutual tasks (1987).

It became clear that the key to performance and productivity would be to have people reduce their dependency on outside authority, trust their own capability to perform, and work together on tasks of importance to the enterprise and to themselves, instead of the dependent alternative of either fighting or withdrawing. Once the environment and task are accurately determined, the goal is then to remove or reduce blockages such as these that distract and demotivate people from doing their work.

Trist and Bamforth, a former coal miner, returned to Bamforth's old workplace to make their profound discovery. To deal with new technical requirements in the mine, the miners had organized themselves into *self-regulating work teams*, with everyone sharing responsibilities and tasks. Trist later wrote about the discovery in a letter:

It was both moving and exciting to talk to the men about the value they placed on their experience in the newly formed autonomous groups. The older miners remembered the very small self-regulating groups of pre-mechanized days and how these had been broken up with bad consequences for them when semi-mechanized longwalls had come in (Emery, 1978).

To emphasize this principal feature of this workplace, Trist created the term *socio-technical system* to characterize the interaction of people (social system) with tools and techniques (technical system). Other key features of this workplace included the following:

- *Technology-induced change.* New technology that supported the work or the worker was the catalyst for change.
- *Teamwork.* Team formation, or "responsible autonomy," as Trist referred to it, encouraged workers to make the decisions about how they would adapt to the new technology. (This system resulted in inherent cooperation between task groups, high personal commitment, low absenteeism, fewer accidents, and higher productivity.)

- *Process-level design*. The level of perspective required to analyze and design work needed to be the entire "work system," rather than Taylor's focus on individual tasks.
- *Whole-systems change*. The entire group of workers, not simply individual workers, needed to be the focus for change.
- *Self-direction*. Internal management of the work system, or "self-directed work," was both necessary and superior in results to external supervision.

Trist, Emery and others continued to study sociotechnical systems between 1949 and 1958, creating an entirely new paradigm for organizing and managing work. (See **Figure 2.3**.) As Trist wrote Emery about his discovery, "I never would have seen the old paradigm for what it was had I not experienced the reality of the new" (Trist, 1977). In search of a humanized workplace such as Taylor had envisioned, Trist and others had pioneered a new set of principles for organizing and managing that were a sharp contrast to classical management theory. Building on new social knowledge unavailable to Smith, Fayol, Taylor and others in the early twentieth century, these new principles focused on the "whole system" for analysis and design, rather than on narrow tasks as Taylor had; and on autonomous work groups, not individuals, as the smallest unit of organization and management. Although their discovery, not unlike Taylor's focus, was based on studies of manual labor, Trist and Emery reasoned that this approach would be all the more important as *knowledge-based work* further dominated the workplace.

Emery introduced Trist and others at Tavistock to the "open systems" concept of Ludwig von Bertalanffy, a biologist (Weisbord, 1987). Bertalanffy's idea was that all things are in some way interrelated and influence each other in all directions, such that cause-and-effect is not the only possible relationship. Relating this concept to organizations and work groups yielded insight that explained many previously observed characteristics. (See **Figure 2.4**.) Taylor, by contrast, had assumed that a company (system) could be isolated and systematized in one best way, regardless of its environment.

And, while some companies were working with sociologists and organizational-development practitioners to apply sociotechnical systems to achieve the advantages they promised, industrial engineers were at work responding to the increasing threats to U.S. manufacturing dominance by learning from the Japanese how to improve production quality.

Figure 2.3
Effective Organizations as Defined by Eric Trist

Old Paradigm *[Early 20th Century]*	*New Paradigm* *[Late 20th Century]*
• Technology first	• Social/technical systems optimized together
• People as machine extension	• People complement machines
• People as spare parts	• People as scarce resources
• Narrow tasks, simple skills	• Multiple broad skills
• External control: procedures book	• Self-control: teams and departments
• Many levels, autocratic style	• Flat organization, participative style
• Competitive	• Cooperative
• Organization's purpose only	• Individual and social purposes included
• Alienation: "It's only a job."	• Commitment: "It's my job."
• Low risk-taking	• Innovation

From Weisbord, 1987, p. 101. (Adapted from Eric Trist, "Adapting to a Changing World," in *Readings in Quality of Working Life*, George F. Sanderson, ed. Ottawa: Labour Canada, 1978, pp. 10-20.)

Quality Initiatives

Following World War II, Japan's industry and labor leaders learned a new set of work principles from industrial engineer Joseph Juran and statistician W. Edwards Deming, American consultants brought in to support the rebuilding of Japan's industry. As a result, Japan achieved astonishing gains in industrial capability and productivity, along with improved living standards for its people. Now commonly referred to as "quality" or "quality function deployment," this improvement initiative applies many aspects of sociotechnical systems theory to the *continuous improvement* of products and services. For continuous

Figure 2.4
Characteristics of "Open Systems"

Characteristics of Open Systems	Description
1. Importation of energy	Organizations import energy from the environment and depend on the environment for such resources/inputs as people, supplies, finances, and information.
2. Throughput	Open systems transform inputs through work processes or methods.
3. Output	Open systems expel the inputs they transformed during throughput into the surrounding environment.
4. Cycle of events	Exchanges between the environment and the organization have a pattern.
5. Negative entropy	Open systems experience a tendency, natural to all organizations, to lose energy and disintegrate.
6. Information input, negative feedback, and the coding process	Open systems receive information in the form of inputs, regulate their operations, and code the information received based on signals to which members of the organization are attuned.
7. The steady state and dynamic homeostasis	The rate of exchange–that is, the general amount of energy expended in receiving inputs, transforming them, and expelling them as outputs–remains relatively constant, in a steady state. The result is dynamic homeostasis, meaning that an even level of activity is attained and preserved in an organization.
8. Differentiation	Open systems are characterized by a movement from general to specialized functions, meaning that there is a tendency for duties or activities to be allocated to different groups or individuals.
9. Integration and coordination	Open systems are characterized by integrative forces that counter differentiation to achieve unity. Coordination assures uniform functioning within the system.
10. Equifinality	Open systems are capable of reaching the same state through many different ways.

SOURCE: D. Katz & R. Kahn, *The Social Psychology of Organizations* (2nd ed.), 1978

improvement, workers at all levels are assigned the responsibility for applying science-based management principles in *solving problems* related to the design of every component of their work.

U.S. industry began to apply these concepts only in the late 1960s, particularly in order to compete with Japan, which at the time produced greater value at lower cost in several industries. In the 1970s and early 1980s, many astute companies launched quality improvement initiatives—targeted improvement programs focusing not only on product and service quality per se, but also on speed, low cost, flexibility and innovation in their core operations—with the ultimate goal of better satisfying customers. Then, in the late 1980s, information systems specialists began to focus management on the potential for reengineering cross-functional processes, making possible significant reductions in the number of unnecessary tasks and workers. To accomplish these quality-improvement and reengineering initiatives, managers began to experiment with teamwork initiatives, finally suggesting *cooperation* over *competition* to better accomplish work.

For companies in the automotive and electronics industries primarily, these changes were part of a determined attempt to stop erosion of their market share—essentially a survival strategy. Many other companies only debated the merits of "quality" and did little to initiate programs of quality improvement. To advocates, quality enhancement was critical for securing and maintaining competitive advantage, then and in the future. To dissenters, "quality" was nothing more than the latest management fad.

By the mid-1980s, quality improvement initiatives had expanded beyond the production floor and point-of-service delivery to incorporate required changes to fundamental management practices throughout organizations. A significant lesson learned in earlier attempts at quality improvement was the need to make supporting changes in areas beyond the factory floor. It was crucial for interrelated organization units and levels to adopt supporting goals in order for the targeted operation to fully realize its quality goals. Performing at higher levels of quality, it was learned, is the result of many integrated factors, including a substantial role for management's basic methods of operating an organization. Many companies responded with aggressive large-scale programs to institute sweeping changes in fundamental management practices throughout their organizations, adopting "Total Quality Management" (TQM) as a metaphor for the new ways in which the company would work and be managed. Although many organizations had attempted similar changes in years prior, usually with limited success, unprecedented competitive pressures now forced this change of fundamental management practices.

Reengineering Business Processes

Whereas quality improvement is based on systematic problem-solving at the task level of work, reengineering takes a more revolutionary approach and redesigns work at the *business process* level. Michael Hammer and James Campy, who pioneered the concept, define reengineering as "the fundamental rethinking and radical redesign of business processes to achieve dramatic improvement in critical measures of performance . . . cost, quality, capital, service and speed" (1993). By focusing on business processes, organizations can redesign workflow and restructure work groups to remove functional barriers, eliminating task-level work, in part, by utilizing today's vastly superior technological capability to support human work.

Successful reengineering yields process and work roles that optimize productivity in much the same way as quality improvement yields tasks that optimize performance. The goals and most of the principles are very similar. The difference is the shift in focus from task-level work (quality) to business-process work (reengineering), and the shift in methods from problem-solving to competitive leadership. Both quality improvement and reengineering will shape the *new work* of the post-industrial organization, and TQM will shape the *new work* of management.

High-Performance Work Systems

Trist and Bamforth's discovery of the interdependence of the technical and social subsystems of an organization may explain why so many TQM and reengineering efforts have stalled. Both of these initiatives focus first on the technical subsystems of work, and engage the social subsystem only as a method to accomplish technical objectives.

By contrast, sociotechnical systems theory provides a different concept for the workplace. This new concept is *not* based simply on the dominance of *technology* or *human relations*, but is based on the "joint optimization" of both the technical and social subsystems, which are considered concurrently and on equal terms. Furthermore, the creation of a joint-optimization design is in the hands of workers—the best source of perception and judgment concerning work. Early attempts to re-create this approach in new and existing worksites enjoyed extraordinary success, with the greatest success gained in *new production facilities* that were designed using sociotechnical principles. In fact, several major U.S. companies used this new workplace concept to earn previously unheard-of profit margins for many years, keeping their strategy a secret for obvious reasons. By the late 1970s, several hundred installations of this design had been completed in the U.S., with a very high success rate (Lawler, 1978).

Based on this experience, several complementary organization design principles emerged (Hanna, 1988; Cherns, 1976):

- *Open systems*. Work system design needs to begin with an "open systems" perspective. Consideration should first be given to the external stakeholders—such as customers, suppliers and competitors—in order to understand the requirements, demands and opportunities of the environment.
- *Few rules*. No more rules than absolutely essential should be specified, providing the maximum latitude for workers to accomplish their work.
- *Source quality*. Quality, or variances, should be controlled at the source, or point of origin.
- *Multiple skills*. Members of the work system should be highly skilled in several functions, so as to make the work system as flexible and adaptive as possible.
- *Process organization*. Interdependent roles within any single process should be within the same work unit in order to maximize coordination and control by workers.
- *Performance support systems*. Information technology should be deployed so that it provides feedback from work processes and other needed information (like task instructions) to the workers making decisions and taking action.

In practice, these concepts lead naturally to the use of "self-directing work teams" to perform and manage interdependent work. The application of sociotechnical design to numerous work systems also leads to other significant changes in organization design (Lawler, 1986):

- *Peer selection*. Employee selection and assignment are based on peer selection.

- *Design participation.* Employees participate in facility design and work configurations.
- *Enriched jobs.* Jobs are based on teamwork and designed to increase autonomy, task variety, and feedback, and to allow workers to complete whole units of product.
- *Skill/performance-based rewards.* Employee rewards are tied to the acquisition of additional skills and the accomplishments of a group.
- *Flat organization.* There are fewer levels of hierarchy, and increased support for self-managing teamwork.
- *Shared vision.* Management is based on a philosophy of partnership aimed at a common vision.
- *Participative decision-making.* Employees receive intensive skills training and work-related education to support their participation in decision-making.

Because of the additional experience in applying, proving and further developing the sociotechnical systems concept gained in the 1980s, we now have a complete view of a *post-industrial organization* design that maximizes the performance and productivity of a workplace. The sociotechnical systems concept is the foundation for what we now think of as "high-performance work systems" (HPWS) (Nadler, et al., 1992) or "high performance organizations" (HPOs) (Hanna, 1988).

According to David Nadler, et al.,

the high performance work systems (HPWS) approach to the design of human work organizations, in its simplest form, is an organizational architecture that brings together work, people, technology, and information in a manner that optimizes the congruence or "fit" among them in order to produce high performance in terms of the effective response to customer requirements and other environmental demands and opportunities.

The HPWS is characterized by 10 core principles. In **Figure 2.5**, these principles are contrasted with the corresponding principles for traditional organization design. Benefiting from more than 20 years' experience with HPWS in the workplace, we can now identify the specific results created:

Figure 2.5
Comparison of Traditional and High-Performance
Work Systems Design Principles

Traditional	*HPWS*
Internally driven design	Customer- and environmentally focused design
Highly controlled fractionated units	Empowered and autonomous units
Ambiguous requirements	Clear direction and goals
Inspection of errors	Control of variance at the source
Technical system dominance	Sociotechnical integration
Limited information flow	Accessible information flow
Fractionated, narrow jobs	Enriched and shared jobs
Controlling and restrictive human resources practices	Empowering human resources practices
Controlling management structure, process, and culture	Empowering management structure, process, and culture
Static designs dependent on senior management redesign	Capacity to reconfigure

From Nadler and Gerstein, 1992, p. 124.

- *Increased quality.* Similar to organizations which have implemented total quality initiatives, HPWS organizations exhibit higher quality in products and services.
- *Reduced cost.* Comparable products and services can be produced, using the same technology, at costs *40 to 50 percent below* traditional methods.
- *Internal motivation.* With workers more responsible for the accomplishment of their work, high levels of ownership are created, leading to increased commitment, discretionary effort, and satisfaction.
- *Self-directed learning.* The increased emphasis on multiple-skill development and worker responsibility leads to greater emphasis on learning and new ideas.

- *Reduced turnover and absenteeism.* Greater involvement and commitment to peers lead to increased job satisfaction and loyalty.
- *Increased flexibility.*   Responsiveness to customer needs, changes in the environment and new technology improves as workers are able to redesign their work processes (Nadler, et al., 1992).

As if operating on a separate challenge — uninvolved in these developments in social, technical and sociotechnical work systems — theorists and practitioners in the fields of instruction and learning have incorporated similar insights into human behavior to advance their discipline.

Development of Instructional Technology

Apprenticeships, on-the-job instruction and classroom education were the chief methods for training in the workplace when Taylor revolutionized employee training. During the twentieth century, instructional technology in effect passed through several "*generations*," substantially changing the instructional practices of major employers and proficient practitioners:

- First generation - Information-based instruction
- Second generation - Behavior-based instruction
- Third generation - Performance-based instruction
- Fourth generation - Learning^2-based instruction

In the early twentieth century, supervisors expert in the knowledge and procedures they taught used information-transfer-oriented methods of instruction. This *first generation* of instructional technology, which was dominant through World War II, was taught by subject-matter experts and based on the theory that people could be adequately prepared for their work by simply giving them as much relevant *information* as quickly as possible, and trusting that they could retain and apply it in their work.   This information was organized logically, sequentially and comprehensibly to maximize knowledge transfer.

In the 1950s, Robert Mager led the shift to a *second generation* of instruction that was based more on specific *behaviors* than on knowledge. Emphasis was placed on helping people prepare to perform their work by identifying the important behaviors in a job and instructing to enable those behaviors. In this generation, knowledge became a means to behavioral outcomes, rather than the goal. The Instructional Systems Design (ISD) model emerged following World War II, arising from the military's development of several standardized teaching methods to compensate for a critical shortage of subject-matter experts during the war (Dick, 1993). This and other models fueled the great expansion of workplace training in 1950s and 1960s because it allowed non-experts to teach.

Then in the 1970s, Tom Gilbert shifted the focus of instructional technology to accomplishment, or *performance*. Founding the *third generation* of instructional technology, Gilbert offered employers a convincing argument that persuaded many that the value of training was not just a change in behavior, but also the achievement of valuable results. This shift in emphasis ultimately led to the reframing of instructional technology into a larger concept—performance technology. In order to provide these kinds of results, it was necessary for instructional designers to consider *non*-instructional methods as well. Attention to the "systems" of an organization became a key factor in achieving performance results, just as it became clear that instruction was frequently not a solution to performance problems.

A *fourth generation* of instructional technology surfaced in the 1960s with the work of Chris Argyris and others who were interested in people's patterns of reasoning, learning and action. Argyris' concept of "double loop learning" (*learning*^{2}) underlies many of the concepts that only in the late 1980s and early 1990s have captured the attention of major employers. This concept represents a new emphasis on the greater capabilities of humans in the workplace, beyond merely taking in and retaining knowledge, adopting behaviors or even performing tasks successfully (1982). This emphasis in effect merges several streams of thought, including cybernetics, action research, educational psychology, andragogy (i.e., adult learning theory) and others, and is now best known through Peter Senge's use of the term "*learning organization*" to refer to a workplace where the goals for instruction go far beyond the bureaucratization of employees to encourage open thinking and communication, learning from mistakes, and a constant focus on confronting reality and making continuous improvements (1990). As it relates to the tasks and roles of work, this fourth generation of instructional technology is referred to as *performance-centered development*, in which the *focus* is work, the *measure* is increased value as determined by the customer, and the *results* are (1) improved work performance,

(2) increased customer satisfaction, (3) new technology, and (4) employee development. Moreover, performance improvement increases employee value, the ultimate determinant of wages.

This newest generation of instructional technology holds the promise to breathe new life into corporate Training functions. Yet many Training practitioners know and use only instructional methods reminiscent of those used in earlier generations.

Corporate Training's New Role

The role of the corporate Training function has changed dramatically since its early days following World War II. Many factors contributed to these changes, including the theories and initiatives in management and instruction described in this chapter.

By 1960, workplace training had begun to have a very different role in organizations. Though training activity was still utilized for the orientation of new workers and for the standardization of important tasks, the principal role and purpose of the Training function had become dissociated from improving task performance and increasing organizational productivity. Training instead had become the preferred method for the continuous, large-scale development of a growing workforce. As new management concepts and theories emerged, organization-wide training initiatives were launched as the primary implementation method for changing workplace behavior. And as new industry regulations and social policies were instituted by the federal government, employees were required to have several hours of training to assure communication of the related issues. More often than not, these often-popular training programs had little or nothing to do with helping employees to learn task skills, perform work or solve problems. They were informational or experiential sessions intended to indoctrinate employees in a common way of perceiving, reasoning or behaving, with the hope of enhancing their development and job satisfaction.

After 1960, the single greatest initiative of most corporate Training departments was employee or human resources development. Particularly in larger companies, this initiative involved an extensive curriculum of training programs, centralized training facilities, tightly managed budgets and, in benchmark cases, even *mandatory* requirements for employees to participate in "X" hours of training per year. Unable to see the results of this strategy and its significant investment, management has placed the future of many corporate Training functions in jeopardy.

Perhaps we need look no further than to Malcolm Knowles, the father of adult learning, to understand why this training-based strategy has not produced the intended result. In *The Adult Learner: A Neglected Species*, first published in 1973, Knowles squarely addressed this failure:

> *The training, teaching or self-development of individuals make[sic] little long-run difference in the productivity, morale, or effectiveness of the organization, and that therefore the energy of the human resources developer should be directed at changing the organization as a total system. Given this definition of the purpose of human resources development, learning and teaching theories geared to individual development are more or less irrelevant; theories of organizational change are what count (1990).*

Clearly, training is needed to acclimate individuals to new organizations and tasks, and to provide knowledge and support skill development. However, astute leaders in the Training field recognize that the greater challenge, and the greater opportunity for corporate Training to add significant value to organizations, is through enhancing the educative quality of the workplace—as in the development of a *"learning organization."* If chosen, this direction will bring corporate Training into alignment with management once again.

Training Is Bypassed

In most organizations, the Training function was passed over by management as the vehicle for providing training to support quality improvement and reengineering efforts. Decisive in this exclusion of Training were the lack of commitment by Training to performance and productivity enhancement, lack of knowledge of broader business issues, lack of support for line management's performance objectives, and lack of vision for its future. Rosabeth Moss Kanter sums up the situation well:

> *Remember that the total-quality revolution was led by industrial engineers, not by human resource professionals — even though the treatment of people, the nature of work systems, and education for problem solving loomed large in the prescriptions of every quality*

*guru. Training and development had the tools, but the engineers
had the vision* (1994).

The industrial engineers who provided the leadership and
strategies for many of these performance- and productivity-enhancing
changes are the same types of people who had implemented Frederick
Taylor's scientific management principles several decades earlier. They
were now taking the logical next step, based on what had been learned
from the successes of the Japanese in rebuilding their industry following World War II. Once the pursuit of quality expanded to the broader
parameters of TQM, adding emphasis on changing both management
practices and corresponding employee work behaviors to support
quality goals, many organizations then brought Training into the quality improvement effort. Training had developed the infrastructure to
support an unending schedule of development activities, the thinking
went, so it would be cost-effective to assign it a major training role.
However, in many companies, this decision only further contributed to
the slow or failed implementation of TQM, as a result of the over-
reliance on training, instead of learning, as the principal method for
producing change.

The Advent of Human Performance Technology

Although it was not obvious at the time—it is difficult to recognize
history in the making—the experience of the past three centuries was
an *evolution* in the science of human work: *human performance technology*. When basic labor was elevated to the mystery work of crafts, it
created value for workers who had special skills. Next, craft knowledge was organized into technology, which disrupted the monopolistic
crafts but initiated the open communication of work methods and gave
birth to the Industrial Revolution. Then to humanize industry, Taylor
pioneered efficient methods for large-scale factories by integrating production technology and workplace economics, and by teaching workers
how to be more productive.

Following World War II, the research of Kurt Lewin and Ronald Lippitt discovered, and Douglas McGregor taught us, ways to
humanize a productive workplace and, as a result, make it even more
productive. More recently, the experiences and further research of Eric
Trist and Fred Emery now compel astute executives, managers and
Human Resources practitioners to radically rethink their approach to

the design of work and the management of organizations. In a time when physical work is being replaced by *knowledge work*, when basic machinery is giving way to *advanced technology*, and when tradition and stability have succumbed to *fast, continuous change*, we now know to adopt a *sociotechnical systems* approach to optimize work performance.

Trist and Emery's view of work was not only extraordinary for its time, but it was also simply not possible in Taylor's day because of limited knowledge of social theory. Now acceptance is growing, much to the benefit of those organizations that are practicing both the methods and the values upon which they are based. This growth is slow, however, because the workplace is filled with many inaccurate perceptions of how to optimize work performance, perceptions that now must be *unlearned*.

We approach a future that will require the achievement of maximum results from people, and this achievement will happen only if we find ways of managing that both employees and the organization they serve will value. To accomplish these goals, there is a pressing need for the organization and integration of existing knowledge in the field of work and human performance. Now, coming from theorists and practitioners in many diverse fields of study, including management, engineering, education, sociology, psychology and economics, a field of human performance technology is emerging. Starting where the evolution of machine technology has taken us, these technologies to enhance human capabilities are emerging as new priorities for competing organizations.

3

Function Follows Form

*In most organizations, both large and small, there is little pressure
from top management to prove that the benefits of training outweigh
the cost. Managers at high levels are too busy worrying about profits,
return on investments, stock prices, and other matters of concern
to the board of directors, stockholders, and customers. They pay little
or no attention to training unless they hear bad things about it.
As long as trainees are happy and do not complain, trainers feel
comfortable, relaxed, and secure.*

Donald L. Kirkpatrick
Evaluating Training Programs (1994)

Between 1880 and 1950, workplace training established its performance-improvement capability by having a dramatic impact on work,
workers and organizations. Training was able to change the way work
was performed by implementing improved work designs throughout
the workplace—improving the capability, behavior, performance and
productivity of workers. The result was improved quality and efficiency in factory work, increased production capacity and industry
productivity, refined products and expanded markets, and added income and an increase in return on investor capital. Simultaneously,
training prepared unskilled and inexperienced people to perform valuable work, and increased the productive value and resulting standard
of living for factory workers. Moreover, training in part enabled the
U.S. to become the pre-eminent economic and military force in the
world.

Then, between 1950 and 1990, the Training function drifted
from its heritage, losing sight of its purpose in the workplace, losing its
capability to improve performance and increase productivity, losing its

credibility with workers and management, and at last losing its value to the organization. This degeneration of the value of training is largely attributable to two factors: the dissociation of training from work itself and the subsequent centralization of training activity into a bureaucratic staff function.

Training Shifts Its Focus

Prior to World War II and for several years thereafter, training activity focused on its intended purpose — teaching work — instructing people on the standardized knowledge and procedures required to perform specific tasks. Following the war, substantial training activity was required to re-integrate veterans into the civilian workplace and to rebuild and expand U.S. industry. Although much of this training involved teaching new task and trade skills for civilian work, much of it did not. Between 1950 and 1970, the definition of training and the use of training methods were expanded to address a much wider range of employee communication, education and development issues.

In particular, training became more broadly utilized by management as a technique for standardizing characteristics of organization behavior that were much less directly related to task performance than ever before. The new objectives ranged from instructing organization members on more-general information, values and behaviors that management wanted to see followed in the workplace, to Training-initiated programs intended to improve member morale, motivation or the quality of workers' lives. Instructional technology was also in its infancy in the early 1950s, including the ISD model, which was then no more than "a collection of processes that collectively were used initially by the military" because there were "too many learners and not enough subject-matter experts" (Dick, 1993).

Notwithstanding the inexperience of Training practitioners at the time, or precisely because of it, training was soon treated as a near-universal methodology for the design of classroom events to ensure communication with employee groups, to change attitudes and behaviors, and to perform cultural transformations. Whenever there was an employee issue, so it seemed, the solution must be training. Practical limitations in Training's capability and effectiveness were ignored. Limited evaluation of the success of such efforts was ever made; management and Training practitioners alike merely presumed that to have exposed people to the communication or experience of training was sufficient.

The shift away from task training to improve task performance and productivity was the most significant change in training activity during this period. This shift was precipitated by several factors, including a reduction in the number of entry-level factory workers requiring training, the piecemeal development of management practice as a discipline, and the support-staff role given to the training function.

Training Becomes a Staff Function

Beginning in the mid-1940s, organizations assigned responsibility for all or most training activity to a Training department, complete with a director and a staff of instructional designers and instructors. In very large or geographically widespread organizations, it was not unusual to find separate Training departments supporting different units of the organization. With a tremendous volume of training activity underway to support the transition and expansion of industry following World War II, many larger firms organized training activity into a staff support function reporting to Personnel, a next-higher-level staff function, and a central unit for handling an organization's people-related obligations. Although this move was consistent with prevailing bureaucratic organizing principles, the impact it would have was not foreseen. Within a few years, this structure—with its disconnection of training activity from its workplace performance and productivity objectives, separation of Training practitioners from the management they were intended to serve, and substitution of function-serving goals in place of business-serving goals—gave rise to Training leadership's loss of focus.

These changes inevitably led to the misuse of training. Such misuse is understandable, as it grew out of the assumptions that training would be required throughout the organization to support all employees for all kinds of needs, rather than retaining its pre-war role of supporting only production and service operations. However, as Training became a separate staff support function, its new objective, characteristic of all bureaucratic staff departments, was to grow in size, budget and political influence. That is one of the well-known games of bureaucratic organizations—the implicit message of bureaucratic compensation schemes: increased activity leads to increased staff and budget leads to increased pay. The resulting goal was more and more *training-like* activity of any kind, regardless of the objectives, investment and likelihood of success. Such a goal only encouraged Training's support of the widespread misuse of training methodology. Training became more concerned with whatever benefited its leaders and practitioners than with the needs of its management customers and organization members. Thus any agenda that supported training-like activity was *inherently good*, and any agenda that did not was *inherently bad*, without regard for the issues involved.

Once the misuse began, the success of the Training department was no longer tied to the preparation of workers to productively perform their work. In many organizations, once there was sufficient development activity ongoing to sustain the department, the technical training responsibility was returned to the operations people because it was not being done to operations' satisfaction—and it was not that much fun for trainers anyway. A consequence of this attitude was a worsening relationship with management.

Management Becomes an Adversary

Despite the success that workplace training had enjoyed since its inception, many Training practitioners rejected this heritage, and with it the objectives of management, when they adopted the viewpoint of the "human relations school" during the 1950s. As discussed in Chapter 2, this viewpoint held that Taylor's principles of scientific management were the predominant source of the limited job satisfaction experienced by workers.

Soon distancing itself from its intended role to support management, Training established its own decidedly normative agenda that was for the most part antihierarchical and at cross-purposes with the views held by line management. In effect, management and its practices became the problem that Training was determined to fix with a continuous list of social and developmental training programs. While emerging science supported the constructs underlying many of these training initiatives, outright attempts to change fundamental management systems through training alone proved fruitless. Management's lack of support for these changes contributed to employees' increasing cynicism toward management and raised doubts about the helpfulness of training.

Senior managers tell me they place some of the blame on Human Resources, Training, and Organization Development units for the early attempts that failed to improve management practices. According to the CEO of a Boston-based high-tech firm,

> *their entire strategy was based on classroom training, yet every-body knows you learn damn little in any classroom. People learn about managing people by understanding the best practices we know, trying them, and then making adjustments as needed. It bothered me at the time we were holding what must have been hundreds and hundreds of classes. I didn't stop it because I wanted to support our people who supposedly knew how we could make the changes we needed. I should have stopped it. Now it's clear, they didn't know what they were doing. They talk a good game plan, but I think that's where it stops. We wasted precious resources, and even worse, frustrated our employees and managers and made everyone skeptical regarding management's ability to lead these changes. Now, we're virtually starting over.*

Bureaucratic Structure

Because the term *bureaucracy* is often used casually or pejoratively, which is not my intent, it is appropriate to take a closer look at the impact of this structure on training activity itself and on the organization of that activity, in order to get to the heart of the dilemma which Training faces.

It is easily appreciated that organizations are important for bringing together varied resources necessary to operate a business or fulfill any mission of reasonable complexity. Of greater significance, however, is the influence that an organization has on its members, which includes (1) providing a context or environment for activity, which supplies much of the coercion that shapes and directs member characteristics and behaviors; (2) providing those responsible the means for applying authority over others; and (3) providing the governing perspective for decision-making by structuring authority and communication. We cannot fully understand the work results of individuals or groups without first understanding the organization in which they work (Simon, 1976).

The principal objective of organization design is to devise a structure that best allows the organization, an entire firm or simply a department to perform its work and fulfill its intended purpose. The resulting activity and success will, to a great extent, conform to the limits of the structure it is given. In design, then, *form* should follow *function*. In application, *function* will ultimately follow *form*.

Consider this example. PBP was recently retained by the senior vice president of Human Resources for a $500 million, 3,200-employee, Midwestern manufacturer of building products to assist in updating the strategic focus, structure and activity of the organization's Training function. The company's Training and Development department reports to Human Resources and is an entirely centralized work unit—its *form*—at the company's headquarters. All training resources, including people and budget and most training activity, are there. Put in place about five years earlier, the design goal of this structure—its intended *function*—was to make sure training support was top quality and equally available throughout the organization, which included operations spread across the U.S. at five small and two large manufacturing plants, twelve distribution sites, sixteen sales and service offices in major cities, and another twenty-five or so salespeople working from home offices.

In the late 1980s, several manufacturing plant managers had complained that they were unable to accomplish their transformation to an empowered and participative workforce because training resources were unequally divided and their on-site Human Resources director lacked the business acumen to meet their training needs. At that time, training people and budget were scattered throughout the organization without any meaningful coordination. Senior management's response was to shift all training responsibility and resources to a centralized director of Training and Human Resource Development reporting to Human Resources. In this way, it was thought, training resources would be equally available and centrally coordinated for everyone's benefit. In application, this structure—the actual *form*—resulted in several mandated, organization-wide training initiatives that consumed most of the Training department's available time and financial resources—the actual *function*—and allowed even fewer individual and departmental training needs to be satisfied than before. Because these major training productions were completed at the direction of senior executives, Training spared no effort or expense to make them spectacular hits with employees, leaving little time and money to focus on the *real* training needs of the organization. In this case, the goal was to improve availability and coordination, yet the highly centralized *form* selected to achieve this goal resulted in a *function* that increased coordination to the point of complete control and even further reduced availability.

Rationale of Bureaucratic Structure

Even though we now recognize that bureaucracies are not perfect mechanisms, as the situation above demonstrates, bureaucracies we·e previously thought of as the ideal organizational structure. As m(·ntioned in Chapter 2, the bureaucracy was the organizational form most widely adopted by companies as they emerged and expanded following World War II. With its extensive hierarchy, divisions of labor, specialized work, formal procedures, and extensive support staff to standardize the work and reduce uncertainty, the bureaucracy was at that time the best way proven to organize work. It was thought to be

> *the embodiment of rationality in the modern world, and, as such,*
> *to be intrinsically superior to all other possible forms of organiza*
> *tions* (Crozier, 1964).

The departmentalization of work into specialties was initially proposed by Henri Fayol in the late 1910s as the best approach for organizing individuals. Fayol's theories paralleled Taylor's scientific management principles regarding the specialization of labor (1949). Max Weber, a sociologist and critic of bureaucracies, coined the term "machine bureaucracy" several years after Fayol defined some of its organizing features. (See **Figure 3.1**.) Notwithstanding his criticism of its subhuman characteristics, Weber saw this form of structure as

> *superior to any other form in precision, in stability, in the strin*
> *gency of its discipline and its reliability. It makes possible a high*
> *degree of calculability of results for the heads of the organization*
> *and for those acting in relation to it* (1947).

Standardization was considered the core principle for designing and organizing work in ever-larger organizations — for dividing work into distinct tasks and then achieving coordination among those tasks.*
Standardization was achieved through the specification of *work* (e.g., procedures, job descriptions), *outputs* (e.g., product specifications, sales

---

* The concept of *mutual adjustment*, in which work is divided and coordinated through communication and other interactions by the people who do the work, is paradoxically suited to both the simplest work, which does not warrant formal coordination; and to highly complex work, which depends on precise coordination under varying circumstances. At this time, organizational growth was adding complexity caused by size alone, rather than as the result of task complexities. This increase in size seemed best handled through increased *standardization*.

Figure 3.1
Max Weber's Characteristics of Bureaucratic Organization Design

#	Characteristic
1	Divide all tasks into highly specialized jobs so people can become experts in their jobs.
2	Have tasks performed according to a system of policies and procedures to ensure uniformity and coordination, and thereby eliminate uncertainty in task performance due to individual differences.
3	Make each person or department of the organization responsible to one and only one manager.
4	Have each employee relate to other employees and customers in an impersonal manner, maintaining a social distance to assure that personalities and favoritism do not interfere with the efficient accomplishment of work.
5	Base employment on technical qualifications and promotion on seniority and achievement.

goals), *skills* (e.g., knowledge, techniques) and *norms* (e.g., mission, values). The alternative concept of *mutual adjustment,* in which work is divided and coordinated through interactions by the people doing the work, was not well suited to the increasing complications inherent in managing a large organization of highly engineered tasks.

Even today, the machine bureaucracy may be the best overall form we know for some organizations. Henry Mintzberg, renowned management scientist and professor of management at McGill University, concludes that

> *when an integrated set of simple, repetitive tasks must be performed precisely and consistently by human beings, this is the most efficient structure – indeed, the only conceivable one.*

Companies ranging from McDonald's to American Airlines depend on the obsession with control to assure strict adherence to practices considered critical for success (1992). McDonald's applies the same "formulas" and work processes at every store location so that a "Big Mac" tastes the same in Oregon as in Massachusetts. American

Airlines must standardize its aircraft service and maintenance function to assure reasonably safe flying.

Role of Support Staff

To develop and refine this mechanical pattern of work, management depends on a large support staff to design and maintain the various systems of standardization, notably strategic plans, operating policies and procedures, job descriptions, rules, regulations, and *training programs*. A current management definition of training activity reveals its continuing *raison d'être* — to meet the standardization needs of the bureaucracy:

> *Training refers to the use of formal instructional programs to establish and standardize in people the requisite skills and knowledge to do particular jobs in organizations. Training is a key design parameter in all work we call professional. Training and formalization are basically substitutes for achieving the standardization (in effect, the bureaucratization) of behavior. In one, the standards are learned as skills, in the other they are imposed on the job as rules* (1992).

Management's support staff is typically organized into separate units by specialization, each having its particular perspective of the organization and a narrow scope of responsibility limited to advising management and administering approved programs and systems. These units are grouped into generally relevant higher-order units, commonly depicted as a hierarchy on organization charts. This grouping encourages coordination by placing related jobs under common supervision to share objectives, resources and measures of performance; and by locating activities to facilitate communication and shared interests.

Following this design, training services were grouped into a single unit of the organization to allow specialization. Furthermore, the Training unit was included with other employee-focused units rather than with the operations units it served, in part because training was perceived to be more closely aligned with the task of hiring new workers than with the principal work of a company. This employee-focused grouping was initially referred to as *industrial relations*, then *personnel* in the 1950s and eventually *human resources* in the 1970s. New-employee indoctrination training, which could easily consist of orientation training, task training and specific skills training, was commonly the first activity new employees engaged in to prepare them for their work. The goal was to have employees fully trained so they could begin work immediately upon taking their positions, and to do so without disrupting the ongoing work or requiring too much special attention from supervisors.

For most organizations, these design parameters have provoked the progressive degeneration and eventual demise of the value-added and effectiveness of Training. Separating Training practitioners from the business units and managers they serve and the workers they train has resulted in a Training function virtually uninformed of changing work and business issues, and fully detached from the performance goals it is to support. In effect, this structure has reduced the role of Training to little more than designing courses and holding classes to present standardized materials to masses of workers—a role that does not meet the needs or cultivate the human-performance potential within organizations today. This may have been just the right approach in 1945, but it is clearly not acceptable for organizations today.

Downside of Bureaucratic Structure

Today, widely shared experience causes most people to use the term *bureaucracy* to describe the negative characteristics of large organizations. These all-too-common expressions of frustration emanate from several characteristics of this still-prevalent form of organization.

Because tasks are divided into separate specialized units that must compete for a share of the total resources, each unit in a bureaucracy is motivated to perceive and interpret situations in such a way that reflects best on itself, and to make its job easier by trying to induce others to change their methods. This is not a question of what is best for the organization, or of the broader challenges faced. In fact, we know from systems theory, with regard to anything separated into parts, that optimizing the parts unquestionably suboptimizes the whole.

Moreover, the people in each unit see from a self-serving perspective, and then act in self-serving ways, regardless of the situation. They experience, decide and act in accordance with their organizational position and whatever management systems are in place to encourage certain behavior. Ultimately, the organizational position of a unit tends to mold the beliefs and attitudes of the people that work in it.

Furthermore, virtually all in-house service and support functions are, in effect, monopolies. They have very little reason to be concerned with their performance, and even less reason to improve it. After all, there is no competition for what they do. Actually, they have a clear disincentive to improve their productivity because of the *games* that staff support functions play.

We all know these games. The first rule is that power and prestige, not to mention income, are determined by the size of staff and budget . . . the bigger the better. Because most support functions cannot really measure a direct contribution to the bottom line, the performance goal becomes *increasing* activities, thereby *expanding* operations and creating excess service capacity. This excess capacity is then used to entrepreneurially advocate various activities that favor the unit until demand is created for more services, which of course will require . . . you guessed it . . . more staff and budget.

Given the interpersonal and entrepreneurial skills of people who lead staff support functions, it is unfortunate that they are all too often unwilling to do the challenging, creative work that is required to make their efforts more productive. It is also not in their best interests. Anyone who knows the game knows that improving efficiency by minimizing staff and expenses is hardly the path to advancement and success in a bureaucracy. It is irrelevant that needless staff-building and budget increases make no business sense; the fact is, *they* made the rules, not you. Furthermore, when staff support functions are criticized for poor performance, the reason is usually attributed to too few resources or a lack of cooperation from the people being served. Needing particular services, management usually responds by increasing staff and budgets.

Keep in mind, too, that working in a staff function is really no way to get ahead in an organization. Because the opportunities are limited, what professionals would want to "bust their knuckles" making some of the tough changes that need to be made? Can management reasonably expect the single-minded dedication, hard work and political risk necessary to really improve performance in an organization? Leadership like this is not likely to happen without some respect. The ablest and most ambitious people know better than to volunteer for the staff support functions, and if they find themselves there, they soon try to get out.

If it will look, Training leadership will find itself at a critical point, on the verge of obsolescence and sure extinction as a staff-support function, or as a future source of competitive advantage. There are extraordinary changes taking place all around Training—in customers, in work, in technology, in organizations, in employees, in management. These developments should suggest the need for changes, dramatic changes, in the corporate Training function.

Changing Needs of the Workforce

The proportion of the U.S. workforce involved in making and transporting products has declined dramatically in the twentieth century, from approximately 80 percent in 1900, to 50 percent in 1950, to less than 20 percent in 1990 (Drucker, 1993). This decline in the number of manual workers has been matched by a proportionate increase in the number of *knowledge workers* and *service workers*, including many entirely new kinds of workers—software programmers, criminalists, healthcare benefits specialists, doctors of nuclear medicine, market research specialists, human performance technologists, media specialists, personal trainers, and so on. Even much of the current work in factories involves the operation of highly sophisticated electronic and precision machinery, not traditional factory labor.

Knowledge and service workers are specialists who must apply their methodologies in combination with other specialists to create valuable output, and who must continuously stay abreast of advances in their methodologies. There are inherent differences in their tasks and associated knowledge and skill requirements, differences which impact their work prerequisites, learning patterns, and training needs. Furthermore, these workers also have substantial demographic, educational and socioeconomic differences, with meaningful implications for appropriate and effective training designs.

The systematic improvement of all knowledge and service work is as vital to U.S. industries and governments today as the redesign of manual work was in the time of Frederick Taylor. Such improvement is the obvious, if not the only, way to improve performance and increase productivity today, since knowledge and service work now accounts for 80 percent of the work in most organizations. However, we have been unsuccessful thus far in our attempts to increase the productivity of knowledge and service workers. The principles for designing, teaching and managing this work have proven to be very different from Taylor's principles for factory work. Achieving these increases has become the central challenge in organizations since 1990, and notwithstanding recent process-focused reengineering and restructuring initiatives, remains a challenge unmet.

Training Today

At present, the Training function is largely ineffective and wasteful, providing little value-added to employees and management, and to the organizations they serve. Today, particularly in larger organizations, employees are required to attend specified training programs along with everyone else or a selected group. In some organizations, employees are required to spend a specified amount of time in training programs or to attend a specified variety of programs each year. In still other organizations, employees can attend any programs they feel will be helpful (or enjoyable), or attend only training programs assigned or approved by their supervisors. Sometimes employees are sent to an apparently randomly chosen training program just because they have had no training in a while; others might be permitted to attend a program because they are loyal to the organization or hardworking and deserve the time off from work.

Lots and lots of training . . . with little perceived effect on performance — and a negative effect on productivity. No wonder employees and management alike are disillusioned with training . . . as they are disappointed with the corporate Training function. Less, not more, work is being accomplished. And somehow, what is learned in class is not the way things really work on the job. Often employees walk out of class wondering exactly what they are supposed to do differently. Or if they have learned better who they are or how they feel about something, they may soon be told that they're still expected to get their work done.

To the point, most training programs wastefully consume resources and reduce worker productivity with endless hours of classtime, and with minimal if any positive impact on worker capability and only rare improvement in performance. It should be no surprise that many Training practitioners receive little recognition from management for anything more than entertaining classroom conduct, just one indication of the low credibility generally attributed to Training practitioners within an organization.

This is not to suggest that all training activity has no value, because some task training (i.e., select technical and professional training) in particular has considerable value to organizations. However, the majority of training provided within organizations provides insignificant value and is woefully inadequate and inefficient in meeting the needs of organizations.

It is significant that Training has played a minimal role in quality improvement and reengineering initiatives, notwithstanding the fact that, in most cases, implementation suffered because of poor handling of the human component. Now, as industry focuses on making further workplace changes to enhance performance and productivity, Training departments in many companies are once again demonstrating their disinterest in this "Machiavellian" kind of activity.

The reasons for Training's decline in value—and its resulting lack of credibility—are complex. Some are external: the shift away from its original focus on task training, and the compartmentalization of Training into a bureaucratic staff function. As discussed in this chapter, however, some of the blame must be shouldered by Training departments and practitioners.

Employees, management, the Training function itself, and organizations have all been negatively impacted by the ways in which Training activity has been carried out in the workplace. But the time for finger-pointing and buck-passing is over. Whatever the causes, the Training function must now reinvent itself if it is to restore its value and regain its credibility—and it can do so only if its goal and its effect are to improve human performance and increase productivity in the organizations it serves.

4

Caught Without Value

*Every three years or so, it is important to sit down with
every staff unit and ask, "What have you contributed
these last three years that makes a real difference to this company?"
Staff work in a business, a hospital, or a government agency
is not done to advance knowledge; its only justification
is the improvement of the performance of operating people
and of the entire organization.*

Peter F. Drucker
The Frontiers of Management (1986)

In a survey of 400 Human Resource Development executives conducted in 1994 by the American Society for Training and Development,
respondents agreed that the number-one trend which will affect the
Human Resource Development field is *the creation of high-performance
work organizations*, which the survey defined as the reorganization,
redesign, and reengineering of work to improve performance in organizations (Galagan, 1994). I certainly would like to have added just
one more question to that survey, something like,

*How are you leading, supporting or blocking your organizations'
efforts to meet that challenge?*

Like me, you have probably read articles in the leading training
publications proclaiming that the Training function is changing to meet
the needs of a changing workplace. Throughout the texts are anecdotal
reports of new programs, methods and, of course, successes. They
contain all the right terms—learning organization, performance, CBT,
CDI, self-directed learning, just-in-time training, Peter Senge, return on

Figure 4.1
"Wake-up Call" Letter to a Client

Dear (Director of Training/HRD):

I've told you frequently what a pleasure it has been to work with you and your organization. That's what makes this a difficult letter for me to write.

As you know, we are having to evaluate many options in our efforts to improve our competitiveness and financial performance. We're paying particular attention to the value added by our various support departments and vendors.

Regarding your organization, I've been unable to present a convincing argument to the Executive Committee. However, all agreed that before we decided to forgo your organization's services in the future, we want to give you the opportunity to prove your value-added to the business. We think that can best be accomplished by having you personally present your case to the Committee.

Let me warn you that specific questions have been raised about the apparent negligible impact of training, as well as the current loss of productivity when our people spend their working hours in a classroom. Then again, I think the Committee is willing to listen to any new approaches you can propose that will measurably improve the company's financial performance.

Please prepare an outline of your presentation that you and I can review beforehand.

Sincerely,

For the Executive Committee

President

investment, competency-based training, performance support systems, and on and on. This is all well and good. But why do I rarely see differences in the ways training is actually provided? Why do Training practitioners refer to management and workers as *they*, not *we*? Why is training designed to win high ratings on a customer service survey rather than to improve work performance or increase productivity? Why do training programs consume all available time and resources, when they could most likely be accomplished with one-half the time and expense? Come on, folks — *where's the beef?*

Many CEOs do agree that one of their major challenges is the creation of a high-performance work organization. However, they do not agree on whether the Training department will be involved, or for that matter, whether Training departments will still exist to witness their organizations' transformation.

Wake-up Call

Take a minute to read the letter in **Figure 4.1** that was received by a client of mine. It is reproduced verbatim, aside from a few words changed to conceal the identity of the company, a Texas-based producer of high-tech products.

This letter was hand-delivered to Molly (not her real name), the Director of Training & Development, at her office, while we were meeting to continue a two-year-long discussion about how Molly's group could increase both the efficiency of its work and the impact of its efforts on the organization. Immediately, the focus of our conversation shifted to the letter and to what she should do next. At my suggestion, we assembled the available department members to discuss the letter and plan the requested presentation. This dialogue, emotional and heated at times, went well into the evening as members dealt with the department's perceived lack of value.

On the following morning, Molly and I met briefly with Todd (not his real name), the CEO, to discuss the group's strategy. It turned out that a strenuous effort to improve the company's operating performance was not hitting its targets, and so a major downsizing was forthcoming. Training & Development was a prime target, but because Molly and Todd had been college friends, she was receiving an added opportunity to make a case to save the department. After introducing me to Todd and discussing briefly how competitive the market had become in recent months, Molly outlined the plan developed by the group.

The group's plan was, for the most part, a summation of improvements that Molly and I had been discussing for almost two years, none of which had been implemented. It called for dramatic changes in Training—changes that would greatly increase the department's ability to support management—including more-comprehensive services with greater impact and lower costs, more on-the-job work-skills training, home-study educational programs in emerging technologies, one-hour team-based work-skills workshops, and many more innovations. Molly had been reluctant to initiate the changes, primarily due to her fear of the department's reaction to the required changes in staffing and work assignments, as well as whatever other problems might arise from such a major change.

Throughout Molly's 15-minute presentation to outline the department's plan, Todd asked just a few questions for clarification and generally listened carefully, while occasionally nodding agreement. Bottom-line, Molly was proposing to lead a revolutionary effort, certainly by Training standards, to measurably improve work performance and increase organizational productivity. This initiative would focus on three key operations of the company—field sales, call-center services and product assembly—all potential areas for establishing competitive advantage. Furthermore, it would be a team effort with management, which would as a by-product equip managers throughout these departments with a working knowledge of the latest developments in *human performance technology*. Molly then pointed out that, armed with PBP's recent assessment of the department's services that identified (1) several areas of considerable value-added, (2) questionable programs yielding little or no value to the company and (3) strategically important programs that could be redesigned for lower cost and greater impact, current training activity was being revised to provide funding for this new initiative and to refund about one-fourth of the department's current budget.

At the end of Molly's presentation, Todd asked a few probing questions, trying to assess realistically the probable success and likely impact of such dramatic changes in the way Training & Development worked within the organization. I offered my understanding of how the group's proposal could be very effective and was able to lend credence to Molly's claims. Much to her credit, Molly rose to the occasion, demonstrating her commitment to lead the changes and her willingness to do whatever it might take to produce the promised results for the organization. She was convincing—you too would have believed that this group could make it happen.

After a brief pause in the discussion, Todd then thanked Molly, expressing sincere appreciation for her and for the group's intention to take on this challenge to benefit the organization. He confessed that he was reasonably convinced that Molly and the department could make a big contribution—in cutting costs and time needed for training, and in improving performance and increasing productivity in several consequential areas of the organization—even though these were unconventional challenges for Training departments, and if successful, they surely would be uncharacteristic results. His remarks were obviously complimentary, and Molly responded with a cautious smile. Todd then paused again, turning sideways to gaze out of the window for perhaps 10 to 15 seconds, although it seemed like several minutes. When he turned back he looked directly at Molly and said,

> *Molly, you need to know how very disappointed I am in you. I mean it. It's a constant struggle for all of us in this company to produce the kind of performance we need to compete successfully. We need every possible advantage just to survive.* He paused briefly. *Only now do I learn that for almost two years you've known how to dramatically improve our performance and reduce your spending.* He paused again, then added, *Why did you wait for me to write?*

Why did you wait for me to write? Molly knew it was a question for which she had many excuses, but no good answer. Surprised, if not stunned, by the question, Molly inhaled as though she was going to offer a response, but then stopped with her mouth open when Todd soon added, *"Thanks for coming in,"* as he waved us out of the office and picked up the phone to place a call. Molly and I returned to a very anxious Training department.

Why did you wait for me to write? Clearly, Todd intended for his question to be a rhetorical way to express his frustration. The significance of the question was profound, however, because it goes beyond the Training department's lack of value to its more critical *lack of credibility.* What typically does not happen in organizations, though, is to have this truth expressed as it was to Molly and me. For the most part, Training is not inclined to raise such a provocative question, not that it would get a straight answer or know how to respond if it did, and management knows there is no reason to speak with such candor until prepared to act. All that's missing is a "business case" —justification based on the needs of the business —to reduce or eliminate Training's resources, and the more competitive markets of the 1990s might just be case enough.

Other Training directors I know would have appreciated the same opportunity Molly had to pitch for survival. Their departments were closed down or severely downsized without notice. For some of these Training directors, it was perhaps their first really clear feedback that all was not well. For years, it seemed, there were always new courses that could be justified, so it became routine to make a persuasive argument for new activity, staff and budget every year. Only in retrospect could these directors now see the signs of the end approaching—their negative attitude that management was the real problem, all the new requests for return-on-investment (ROI) figures for seemingly sacred training programs, less contact from management and less advance information on the company's business plans, and quite a bit more resistance to the time required for people to attend courses. But until they got the ax, these Training directors believed the game would go on forever.

Just Say *No*!

I was astonished, at first, on the day in 1992 when a large company that I was very familiar with announced the cancellation of all training programs and elimination of the Training function. Even programs scheduled to begin on the very next day were cancelled. Programs in session at the time the word was passed down were stopped immediately. The memo was all too clear:

> *Until further notice, all training activity is cancelled.*
> *This cancellation includes internal programs, vendor-supplied programs, industry and trade conferences, and any other examples you can think of.*
> *All training currently in progress is to be cancelled immediately, and all individuals away from the company at training events are to return to work at once.*
> *There will be no further training without senior executive approval, and approval isn't likely for the foreseeable future!*

Clearly, the frustration of the deciding executive is evident in these words. A subsequent discussion with him clarified that repeated attempts to increase the impact and cost-effectiveness of training activity had resulted in only half-hearted efforts and no real change. The company's financial performance had weakened considerably in recent years, and management was feeling strong pressure to dramatically improve sales and profitability. The executive committee and line managers agreed that training clearly played an important role in improving the capability of the organization and would be a major player in establishing competitive advantage in some key service areas. At the same time, they were frustrated in their failure to utilize Training to improve business performance.

The memory of this event may have passed quickly for most, but I would wager the Training staff will remember it for a long time. What the memo only hinted at was the resultant swift demise of the Training function. A few top practitioners from the Training staff were transferred into manufacturing and distribution operations areas to support important basic technical skills instruction, and a few others were offered positions in which their talents could be re-employed. Employment of the others was suddenly terminated.

As I later learned, numerous companies, large and small, were taking similar action to end Training's perceived waste of resources and unresponsiveness to management's concerns. Many were very large, and several maintained worldwide operations. At first, these changes seemed to me to be drastic and potentially short-sighted. I know from my consulting work that most CEOs realize that the performance of the organization is going to make more and more of a competitive difference in the years ahead. Knowing the demands of the global marketplace, and acknowledging that Training must be involved if an organization is to succeed, what would prompt CEOs to take such seemingly radical action? How were these organizations going to develop their people? How were they going to improve human performance so that they could remain competitive or develop a competitive advantage? Each situation was slightly different, certainly, but the common element seemed to be a high level of frustration that had been reached by *both* management and the Training staff. Both had tried what they knew to do, but without success. The goal at this point was simply to *end the misery* for everyone involved.

Training's Inadequate Response

Scenarios such as these show clearly that the Training function is at a crossroads that will determine its future. Some say that Training is at the mature stage in its life cycle — that it will either die or reinvent itself as a potent force in organizations. Others claim that Training is already changing to meet the emerging needs of organizations, but perhaps it needs to make these changes more apparent. Still others just do not get it. They do not recognize the irrelevance and the waste, but they will soon be *caught without value.*

Unfortunately, most Training departments have instituted only minor changes in their regular programs and related support activity in response to this period of great transition. And the most common changes I find simply entail the addition of courses to teach the new topics of discussion, such as teamwork, empowerment, surviving downsizing, and so on. It is rare that I identify a Training staff really concerning itself with the operating performance of the business, trying hard to *really* help workers improve their performance, or attempting to have a greater impact on improving the bottom line.

Why have Training practitioners generally not focused on performance and the bottom line? Many in Training have misconceived discoveries in the social sciences as ends in themselves, failing to remember that the management of organizations is fundamentally an economic activity. As a result, new human-relations concepts took on an importance of their own, often without profitable connection to the organization they were to serve. Development programs were sponsored for vague reasons unconnected with the economic concerns of the organization. When the concepts of the training were not supported by management, organization members became disillusioned and Training practitioners characterized management as the villain. This duplicity toward management has caused the Training function to lose credibility with management and has limited the value-added perceived for training services.

Another reason for Training's lack of value is that for years, most Training directors have claimed to have too few resources. Either they have too few people to adequately keep up with the volume of programs demanded by their customers, or their budgets are so tight that certain new vendor programs cannot possibly be added to the curriculum. The justifications for increases typically include the number of programs offered, class days held, participants served, and so on.

The basic concern is, then, how to do more so they can get more. This is typical bureaucratic thinking.

Need for New Thinking

In most organizations, this kind of thinking cannot continue. Rather, internal service providers have to ask themselves how they can have the greatest positive impact with the fewest resources. In other words, an organization can afford for Training to provide only services that make an obvious contribution to business performance, whether short or long term, and these services need to be provided in the most efficient manner possible. Anything less is a disservice to the organization and its members.

Clearly, this is a new way of thinking for most. It may be rare, although not unheard of, for a Training director to voluntarily announce the curtailment of training activity due to its minimal impact and value-added. Rarer yet is the Training director who voluntarily reduces staff or budget because of new efficiencies. Though perhaps rare today, this is the Training director of the future. Any other approach to this role is an attempt to favor the Training function at the expense of the organization, its management and its members.

Once adopted by Training's leadership, this perspective quickly uncovers many opportunities to reduce waste. Some of the bigger opportunities that are also reasonably easy to seize are (1) the quick elimination of unnecessary or non-priority training programs, (2) the elimination or redesign of training programs that simply do not work, (3) the relatively simple redesign of all training programs to increase their impact and results, and to reduce their time requirements and cost by one-half or more, and (4) the standardization of duplicate programs across the organization.

Reestablishing Value

People will always be needed to do the work of producing and transporting products–traditional factory work—but this is not our challenge. Today's workplace training must go beyond simply instructing employees how to perform narrowly defined tasks. Rather, the greatest training need, now and for the next 20 years, is to produce technician-level knowledge workers and service workers. These people now make up 80 percent of our labor force, yet their performance is generally unacceptable by competitive standards. There is an urgent need to bring these people to a higher level of skill, consisting of both a formal understanding of the sciences and technologies related to their roles and a self-directed capability to continue learning. Whether analyzing complex issues, operating sophisticated equipment, performing delicate manual procedures, servicing valuable clients or simply being responsible for important matters, these specialists must be ready to assume much broader roles and responsibilities than ever before, including imaginative thinking, intra-organizational cooperation, and discretionary effort.

Will the Training function be the vehicle for meeting this challenge, or will the torch be passed to others who can deliver what is needed to support the learning and relearning required of this growing cadre of knowledge and service workers? Has Training heard the wake-up call? If so, are Training departments willing to make hard choices soon enough — as Molly had not done? Or will they see their departments dismantled and their jobs eliminated?

The state of corporate Training is nothing less than a crisis for many organizations. The self-disclosing Training director would, in most cases, have to admit that he or she has developed neither the strategy nor the relationships to direct Training to be what it needs to be if it is to support today's post-industrial workforce and the managers responsible for organizational performance.

Subsequent chapters will address ways to develop these appropriate strategies. And the challenge to build truly supportive relationships with all employees, managers and corporate executives should be facilitated by the excellent relationship-building skills of most Training practitioners — that is, once they align their loyalties with their responsibilities.

Part II

Paths for Change

To abandon anything is always bitterly resisted.
People in any organization, including bureaucrats and politicians,
are always attached to the obsolete; the obsolescent;
the things that should have worked but didn't;
the things that once were productive and no longer are.

> Peter F. Drucker
> *Post-Capitalist Society* (1993)

I routinely talk with chief executive officers, and I am frequently reminded of my amazement when I first realized that many of them often feel that they are the only people in their organizations who are fully concerned with the performance of the entire enterprise. Notwithstanding CEOs' efforts to develop a shared view of the organization's purpose, values and goals, everyone else is concerned for the most part with his or her specific area of direct responsibility, whether it's a subsidiary, business unit, division, function, department, section, role, or project. This prevalent attitude of individuals with different responsibilities is accurately described as competitive — all competing for resources to improve their situations, and potentially to maximize their performance, make their lives easier, or otherwise have things go their way — and such an attitude frequently works to the detriment of the entire organization. In fact, as mentioned previously, optimizing the parts of a whole will by necessity sub-optimize the whole.

We can attribute this result to institutional factors. The bureaucracy — the principal organizational form since the 1950s, plus incentives for individual accomplishments, and compensation systems rewarding staff and budget size, have encouraged and supported this intra-organizational competition. Perceptive individuals would quite naturally be motivated to promote their piece of the organization, even to promote it when it did not serve the organization's best interests, and possibly to promote it to the point that this effort would prove detrimental to other pieces of the organization, and to the entire organization.

Why Couldn't Training . . . ?

The Training function has been managed this way, but is probably no more or less self-serving than the other staff support functions in organizations. Training management's goal has been to build a training empire, so to speak, and to do so they have promoted training as a solution that is well beyond its capability. Training directors have continuously looked for defensible ways to expand their departments' workload, staff and budget by increasing the number of programs offered, the facilities and equipment required, and the number of instructors on staff. To support their cause, they have promoted favorable ways to measure and demonstrate achievement, such as number of programs offered, total training days, number of participants and favorable participant evaluations.

In the course of this pursuit, the Training function has lost sight of its purpose, has focused on activity that wastes resources and reduces productivity for the organization, and has failed to fulfill its promise of improved performance to organization members and management. Some of the more effective current applications of training, including programs to teach the tools and techniques for quality improvement and reengineering, do not even involve the Training department. These programs are more often taught by managers, fellow employees, industrial engineers or trainers working within operations.

Now on the verge of irrelevance, the Training function must either develop and deliver high value to the organization, or risk elimination. And, of all the ramifications of such a choice, the most critical one is the possible loss of the potential value to the organization that is inherent in so many Training practitioners—specifically their interest, knowledge, skills and acumen in developing the capabilities of people—a value that today remains unrealized.

When asked for the ROI of training, Training departments go *crazy* trying to produce a formula, set of data or other evidence that provides unequivocal proof of the investment return on their training activity. Unfortunately, the point of the request is being missed. Managers rarely, if ever, make decisions based on ROI; such burdensome calculations are appropriate for multi-million-dollar capital expenditures, not training programs. What managers are saying, albeit too indirectly, is that they lack confidence that the training activity in question does in fact add significant value to the organization. Perhaps managers have learned that they have to ask for facts in order to get a logical response from Training. They know that staff support services are in the habit of quickly jumping into a defensive routine to justify their existence. Intuitively, they lack confidence in the value of training programs, and are rightly asking for a rational confirmation of the training activity's value to the organization.

If such value exists, it can be represented by comparing the estimated value of the three most important results of the training to the total investment required (including participant time off the job); the well-accepted formula for ROI is "output value divided by input cost." Since managers naturally want to work with people they can trust and who approach business maturely, the correct response might sound more like this:

What's your concern? Good idea. We haven't assessed the value of this program in several years. When do you need the figures? Do you have a minute to discuss what you see as the specific costs and results of the training? I'd like to start with your figures if you have some. Do you have any other concerns that we might research at the same time?

If the calculations using the output/input formula show that the training program offers significant value to the company, then that fact should be presented unemotionally and the figures explained. The same approach should be used if the calculations show that the program does not offer value. When I have been involved as a consultant in circumstances such as these, I find that management is just doing what management is paid to do: assure that the organization is making the wisest use of its investments. It is counterproductive for everyone when Training takes a defensive posture.

Wouldn't it be admirable to see Training leadership rise to this challenge rather than defend its current activity? Why couldn't Training strive to do what is best for the business—focus on the business needs first so as to determine the real performance-improvement needs of organization members and then support them in the best way possible, even though this approach might reduce the quantity of training activity? This strategy would surely identify considerable work for which Training practitioners are uniquely qualified within the organization. All that is needed is a broadening of Training's roles, goals and capabilities.

Try Leadership

To share the CEO's concern for business performance, one first needs to know the metrics, or relevant performance measures, that apply. When Training's focus is the business, then it is no longer necessary to create new measures, like participant days or program evaluations, to argue the worth of training activity. The business already has effective measures, and Training simply needs to know the ones to which management assigns more importance. Though there may be some variation due to industry- or market-related issues, or simply personal preference, there are five measurements that experienced executives commonly use to determine how the overall business is doing:

1. Market share
2. Innovation
3. Productivity
4. Cash flow and liquidity
5. Profitability

Take note that "short-term earnings" is not listed; it is not a reliable indicator of business performance. Though quarterly earnings have long been thought to be the only indicator senior executives were concerned about, these figures are dubious, if not misleading, indicators to management of the performance of the business. Though most experienced executives know this, they nonetheless have to appease investment analysts and asset managers who react rather impulsively to quarterly earnings reports, and on whom the business depends for favorable investment press, favorable stock performance, and ultimately favorable regard by investors for the stocks and other financial instruments with which the company finances its operations.

Next, it is necessary to know what these measures mean, how they are calculated, what the source of accurate data is, why they are important, and what benchmarks or standards management applies. Asking for this information, if it has not already been provided and simply neglected, may turn a few heads in the organization, but it also sends the right message. It is important to find out what these figures mean if it is not immediately obvious how various kinds of changes would raise and lower them. For example, "market share" indicates the proportion of a product's or company's sales to a market's total sales, and it is calculated by dividing total market sales by the company's sales in the same category. Research has shown that greater market share generally yields many advantages — a principal one being higher profitability because of the lower costs associated with higher-volume marketing, production and service activity. Market share is raised by adding customer value to products and services in the form of improved performance for the consumer, higher quality and reliability, more satisfying customer service, and lower purchase and usage costs.

This kind of information can be used to plan the work of the Training department. How? The department can identify which measures are currently the greatest concern to management, as concerns will vary with the company's circumstances. Because human-performance improvement can impact all five measures — although not with the same amount of effort, time and investment — one needs to develop a plan. Generally speaking, the goal should be to create the greatest value, and to do it in the least time possible and with the least possible investment and risk. If management's top priority is to establish a competitive advantage to increase market share, then a plan might be proposed for working with the service delivery organization to improve the customer satisfaction rating, and to reduce turnover and improve the cross-selling performance of the customer-service center. Alternatively, if management's immediate need is cash, training could propose an all-out effort to reduce the cost of mission-critical training, temporarily set aside all other programs, and then focus the Training staff on various performance problem-solving projects that would reduce other operating costs. In some organizations, such a dramatic change from the traditional role of Training will require the initiative or sponsorship of a senior executive.

One of my goals for this book is to provide Training leadership and practitioners insight on ways to direct the rethinking and ultimate restructuring of the Training department, rather than waiting for management to become sufficiently frustrated to make these changes for them. In Part II, I use two examples in the form of vignettes from the experiences of client companies to illustrate this kind of leadership. The first example, in Chapter 5, "Free Cash Flow," focuses on an organization under short-term financial pressure and therefore needing to maximize cash flow and profitability. The second example, in Chapter 6, "Commitment to Change," focuses on an organization caught in the games that organizations play. It illustrates these all-too-common activities, as well as the most likely way they will be successfully resolved. Both vignettes are based on actual situations, which I selected for their familiar circumstances. Concepts and techniques for developing superior human performance and improving the effectiveness and efficiency of training programs will be introduced, but the details on how these tools work are presented in later chapters.

The reflective reader will go beyond these two examples to consider the many possible circumstances and appropriate responses for which these are merely examples. Since every organization's circumstances are unique, it is wise to weigh more heavily the issues that are more relevant, valid and compelling for a particular organization. Training leaders especially need to expand their methods and capabilities well beyond classroom training, and need to align themselves with management and directly support the achievement of management's objectives. Training practitioners need to expand their repertoires and become skilled in related interventions that enhance learning, performance and productivity; and that directly support management. I find that once people accept the premise that Training is not currently fulfilling its implicit promise to improve human performance in the workplace, they will begin to recognize and consider these many new alternatives.

5

Free Cash Flow

There are various reasons for making changes, even when not absolutely forced to do so: the desire to be an industry leader, the desire to continually improve performance and increase profitability, the desire to improve the quality of work life, even the fascination with innovation itself.

Gerard Egan
Adding Value (1993)

Today we read about and engage in considerable talk about *alignment* — the condition of allying oneself with one side of a cause . . . being in an alliance with another person such that both views support a shared objective. The term *alignment* does not suggest that one person or the other does not have his or her own views . . . rather, that there is general agreement on the objective or purpose, and support in the form of defense, assistance or advocacy. For business, the metaphor that is most meaningful for me is a "tug-of-war." In a tug-of-war, alignment is a matter of being on the same side . . . the same end of the rope. The test for alignment, then, is that if you are not pulling with me, essentially you are helping the other side. Today, there are even seminars about alignment. You might have received brochures for, or even attended, seminars titled, "Aligning Training with the New Corporate Agenda" or "How to Align Human Resources with Corporate Strategy." It's a hot topic. Why?

The reason we now hear so much more about alignment is that it has now become important to business survival and success. Competitive pressures in most industries make it impossible for a business to survive and compete unless every division, department, role and activity of the organization is working cooperatively toward the same overall goal. For years, before global competition was a reality, organization members could afford to engage in bureaucratic gamesmanship—building empires of staff and services to enhance their political influence—and the business could survive simply by passing on these valueless added costs to customers. Not so today. Now, every bit of cost must add value, and the goal has to be for all costs to add the greatest value possible. Nowadays, even service costs that add value are being cut because they are competing with other service costs that add even greater value. The question faced by corporate Training or any other service provider, whether internal or external to the organization, is how much *more* value training activity adds as compared with alternative services, not just that training adds value or even that it adds value equivalent to its costs.

Alignment is so important now because it is critical to value generation. Today, 100 percent alignment with management—complete support for and advocacy of the achievement of management's objectives—is the only sensible goal for Training and for other staff support services as well. Furthermore, staff support services add the greatest value when they are exactly what the circumstances warrant. A service is out of alignment to the extent that it is not 100 percent effective in doing what is needed to support management. Having to compete in today's exceedingly competitive markets, businesses can no longer afford the misalignment that has become characteristic of large bureaucratic organizations.

Moving Forward

Let's use the example of a billion-dollar Midwestern manufacturer of construction and consumer durable products. Rick joined the company two years ago as the Director of Organization Development & Training (OD&T). The company was a great place to work—good pay, great benefits, well-known products, friendly people, solid Midwestern values, etc.—and the department was in great shape, with a budget of more than $4 million, a competent staff of developers, trainers and organization development consultants, and aging yet fashionable facilities.

Recently, he attended one of those "alignment" seminars, and it sent him home with a number of apprehensions. It struck Rick that in the presentations—most of them made by the directors of Training for other big-name companies—none of the presenters seemed to be really concerned about the companies they worked for. Virtually all of them spoke about what was good for Training, not what was good for the business; they spoke about how many programs they offered and how many participant days they trained, about the extravagant equipment they convinced management to invest in, about how to justify and prove the worth of training programs to management, and about ways to "fix" management so training could have greater impact. Rick reasoned that the presenters mirrored his own thoughts, and such a discovery was particularly unsettling to him because there was something capricious, if not downright irresponsible, about their words. Rick was troubled by his observations.

Only a month beforehand, Rick and I had met accidentally at a management conference at which I was speaking and he was attending in place of his supervisor, the VP of Human Resources. Now, he was calling me for guidance, and soon thereafter we met to discuss his concerns and consider how he might best resolve them. Key among these were the following:

1. *Management's concerns*

   The seminar stimulated Rick's thinking about the business that his centralized department was there to serve and support, and in particular about the business issues most troubling to management. His first concern was that he did not know with any certainty what management's concerns for the business were. He could not remember the last time he had had a discussion with a senior manager about that manager's business. It seemed as though any recent discussions with management had been about training programs or Rick's business, and not about the business that really mattered. Discussions with his supervisor were always about Human Resources department concerns or specific projects and programs. Rick soon realized that his self-focus was keeping the whole department focused on its own issues . . . not the more important management issues. How was anybody in the department to know what management's real concerns were if he, the director of the department, did not secure this knowledge for the entire department's benefit? He knew that the real issues of the company weren't going to show up in the company newsletter or quarterly report to shareholders; he would learn management's concerns only by discussing them at every opportunity.

2. *Feedback on value-added*

   Rick's was also concerned about feedback from the organization about the effectiveness of the department's services. His two annual reviews were very complimentary; training program participant evaluations had been consistently favorable; people were always complimenting him for little things he did or said; and the staff frequently received "attaways" for its work. But he wondered whether any of this really mattered. Again, Rick was smart enough to realize that even with all that feedback from the organization, he was not learning what he really needed to know from his customers—the senior managers for the major operations of the business. Rick was beginning to figure out that the bottom line was whether the OD&T department was adding significant value to the business, and what he desperately needed to know was how the department could add even more value.

3. *High-value-added services*

   Rick's lack of substantial information on the value-added by the OD&T department raised for him some bothersome questions about the department's services. He pointed to the department's inch-thick, professionally bound course catalog sitting on his desk and remarked, "This is what we do here. I wonder if any of it makes a difference. Is this really what the organization needs? Are we doing all we can to help management, to help employees do their work? I hate to say it, but I'd be hard-pressed to describe any positive outcome from all this activity and expense." As Rick fanned through the catalog, shaking his head in apparent disgust, I remember asking him, in hopes of pointing out some positive impact the department's work was having, to tell me about any tough problems the department had been able to help one of its customers resolve. My strategy backfired on me and simply reminded Rick of management challenges about which OD&T was doing nothing.

4. *Customer focus*

   "Customers? What customers? We don't have customers; we just offer services for anybody who wants what we offer." Rick pointed out that the department's efforts to focus more specifically on the needs of the major units of the organization had failed miserably. He was uncertain why the department had failed, except that the department members who volunteered for an added assignment to build a link with customers were unsuccessful at striking a collaborative relationship with these managers. He guessed that, as knowledgeable and professional as these staff members were, they did not have enough credibility in the organization to gain the attention and serious interest of these managers, enough business experience to really appreciate and purposefully discuss a manager's problems, or enough breadth in resources and organizational influence to substantially effect a solution to a manager's real predicament. The staff recognized these shortcomings, but lacked the confidence to converse outside these limits. Thus another concern surfaced.

5. *Limited capability*
Rick told me about his experiences as he had worked his way up the ladder in two prior training-and-development assignments for other companies, concluding with the endorsement of his current staff as the highest caliber of practitioners with whom he had ever worked. He went on to elaborate that of his direct staff of 28 professionals, including designers, developers, instructors, OD consultants, and four administrative assistants, all but eight were college-educated, twelve had master's-level degrees in either teaching or a social science, most had attended seminars and workshops on various aspects of training and development, and ten had worked for four or more years in other staff units of the company before transferring to OD&T. Rick asked rhetorically, "What's wrong with this picture?" He answered his own question while counting off on his fingers: "No business education, no operations experience, no marketing experience, no financial experience, no significant management experience, no industrial engineers, no systems people, no customer service people—it's as though we are operating with this incredibly narrow-minded view and corresponding limited capability to impact the success of this business."

Though one might easily think Rick could have continued directing the OD&T department just the way he had been for the past two years, it was clear to me that he could not. The influence for this change was originating not from external forces, but from Rick alone. While talking with him, I was reminded of a concept I refer to as "the one-way bridge" that I learned from Pat Williams, a management professor and philosopher who founded the extraordinary M.S. in Organization Development program at Pepperdine University. The idea is that once we come to know something—once reality moves into our conscious minds—we cannot send it back to pre-consciousness. Rick's paradigm had changed; now that he was asking these pertinent questions and knew their disquieting answers, he could not abandon this perception; he had to do something about it. Furthermore, by discussing these issues with me, however unsettling it may have been for him, he clearly exhibited the courage to take some action in response. Then well into our conversation he posed the question, "What do you think I should do?" It was clear that Rick was operating in unfamiliar territory, so I sketched out a simple three-step plan to move him forward.

First, I recommended that Rick have the same discussion with his supervisor that he was having with me. He had spoken highly about her throughout our meeting, and she would certainly have insight for him that I could not provide about the company and its management. Besides, it was important to keep her informed before taking this next step. My second recommendation was that he talk personally with the 20-odd business unit and major function managers located at headquarters, and subsequently by phone with senior managers in other areas of the U.S. and the world. I suggested he invest some time before these meetings in determining what he really wanted to know from these people, and make it his goal to be listening to them about 90 percent of the time. To help, we agreed he would even send them a memo beforehand outlining his questions. Third, I recommended that he bring his staff together for a weekend retreat to present his concerns, the feedback he would receive from management, and the basic questions he felt were facing the department in regard to its future.

Rick's immediate response was understandable—he was at once skeptical about making his concerns known within the company, and energized about the good prospects inherent in pursuing them. He wondered how open-minded and supportive management would be, and in what kind of jeopardy he might be placing his job with the company. We reasoned that this approach was focused on gathering meaningful business information, not about admitting failure. Ultimately, I think his achievement drive outvoted his apprehension, and he said he would follow my suggestions. He also asked me to join him in meeting with his supervisor and assist him in designing and facilitating the weekend retreat with the OD&T staff. As it turned out, we were able to meet with his supervisor the very next morning. Providing both relief and assurance, the meeting went well. She encouraged Rick to follow through on the suggestions and offered to provide whatever assistance she could.

Rick claims to have learned more than he could ever imagine knowing about his company's business in the 45 days following our meeting. Throughout this whirlwind of activity, Rick learned all about the company's major businesses, products, production capabilities, service programs, financial performance, forthcoming innovations, and pressing problems. Most of his meetings with management led to follow-up meetings, facility tours, strategy briefings, and additional interviews with key managers not on his list. Rick's supervisor even arranged for Rick to have 45 minutes with the CEO, whom Rick had never before met. Rick's inquiry became a crash course on the people and issues of the business.

In preparing for the retreat, Rick decided that he wanted to focus, not on the long-term future of OD&T, but on what the department staff could do within the next six months to contribute the maximum possible value to the business. That would be an initial test to see if the department could in fact make a positive difference. Of particular interest was that the company was facing a serious cash shortage arising from a combination of unforeseen events, including the loss of two major government contracts, a late new-product introduction, a failed attempt to increase prices, excessive start-up costs in Eastern Europe and several other factors — all draining the company's cash unexpectedly. The severity of the situation was not widely known in the company because any resulting publicity would potentially impact the pricing of a secondary stock offering the company was planning for the following quarter. A number of alternatives to minimize the problem were under consideration, including budget cuts, a hiring freeze, staff reductions, and plant consolidations with layoffs.

Rick selected for the retreat one of the company's manufacturing facilities five miles from town. Between the cafeteria and some picnic tables outside, we had all the space and quiet we needed to work. Furthermore, all the participants could return to their homes in the evening. It doesn't get any less expensive than that. And, since most members of the staff had not been in this plant — or any company plant, for that matter — the atmosphere provided some reality about what the company was all about.

The retreat was kicked off with a casual dinner on Friday evening, and it is no overstatement to say that Rick held the staff spellbound after dinner by telling the entire story of the events that had led up to that evening. Everyone stayed in the group discussion until long past 10:00 p.m., asking questions, talking and otherwise trying to get used to the ideas that Rick had presented. Let me summarize the remainder of the retreat, which at times involved some very heated discussion, by outlining the plan that the staff unanimously adopted before ending the retreat at 4:00 p.m. on Sunday afternoon. The department still needed the support of Rick's supervisor, but everyone was confident it would be given. These were the key elements:

- *Timetable:*
  To begin immediately (May) and continue through December. Emphasis on immediate value-added.

- *Goal:*
  Maximize value-added to the company, without restriction to traditional training activity. Emphasis on increasing productivity and reducing costs so as to increase profitability and thus help satisfy the company's need for free cash flow.

- *Objectives:*
  1. Return $1.65 million of OD&T's non-payroll budget—$1.1 million in training program costs and $.55 million in discretionary operating expenses.
  2. Eliminate 20,000 employee days of lost productivity—approximately $5 million in recovered value.
  3. Reduce manufacturing and distribution costs by $22.4 million—$2.4 million in eliminated training costs, and $20 million in operating costs.
  4. Launch a "performance improvement" unit to which management could turn for assistance in solving people-related performance problems.
  5. Meet management requirements for "how to" training in performance-improvement methods.

- *Action Plans:* (a partial listing)
  1. Have OD&T staff eliminate all non-essential expenditures. (honor system)

2. Identify and temporarily suspend all training activity that is not mission-critical. *— Within one week*
3. Redesign all mission-critical training to reduce class time and costs by 50 percent or more.* *— Within ten weeks*
4. Develop a "performance improvement" unit within 'he department, staff it with the more capable "consultanus," and augment the group with specialists from throughout the company (e.g., information systems, industrial engineering, finance, accounting and human resources) to support management in dealing with people-related performance problems.† *— Within six weeks*
   Provide evening and Saturday open-enrollment "crash courses" in (a) personal performance improvement, (b) learning, (c) modern work practices (e.g., time, project, and people management), (d) process and work improvement, and (e) cycle-time reduction, in addition to other performance-improvement training programs judged helpful by management. *— Within four weeks*
5. Seek out situations in which human-performance improvement would increase productivity, customer satisfaction, or both, and work with management to facilitate needed changes to capitalize on these opportunities. *— Within twelve weeks*

Take note — this was not a training plan; it was a performance-improvement plan, it was in alignment with the company's needs, and it specified training activity only where it would produce the needed result. The OD&T staff demonstrated my often-repeated experience at similar functions — no matter how radical the changes required from a Training department, it is able to "cross the bridge" into a whole new paradigm for the Training function if it puts the staff in charge of the response.

The importance of this vignette lies in the responsive leadership of the Training function it portrays. Very similar to the situation in which many Training practitioners find themselves, it suggests a strategy that simply tries to be helpful and value-adding. And to do this well, it suggests breaking out of the limitations of instruction,

---

* See Chapter 14, "Training — Better, Faster, Cheaper," for additional information on the Training Redesign process for improving the cost-effectiveness of training.
† See Part IV, "Training Gets to Work," for more insight into developing a "performance improvement" unit like the one outlined here.

development and programs to work with clients and assist them in ways that will make them successful.

You may be interested to know that Rick's supervisor did approve the plan as submitted, and furthermore supported the staff's efforts throughout the year and throughout the trials and tribulations that ensued. Keep in mind that Rick was initially the only "inner-driven" member of the staff; while everyone bought on to the plan, many did so with a mixture of enthusiasm and trepidation. All things considered, the OD&T staff was remarkably successful in implementing its strategy. To the surprise of many, including staff members, the financial targets proved to be very practical goals. At year's end, it was obvious to everyone involved that the entire effort required the cooperation of other staff functions, the operating units and senior management, so much so that credit for this achievement had to be attributed to everyone involved.

With the cash crisis securely behind the company—the real achievement—Rick's supervisor sponsored a luncheon to acknowledge the OD&T staff's efforts and invited everyone who was involved and could make it to the event. Having been invited myself, I enjoyed the opportunity to see Rick recognized so appreciatively by everyone, and to hear his remarks to the group. He told the same story about how it all started at the "alignment seminar," talked about the retreat, pointed out who and what he was most proud of, and then thanked all involved for their hard work and contribution to the company. He then closed his brief talk, looking out among the admiring guests, with his eyes moistened by heartfelt emotion, with these fitting words, which I still remember:

> *It was courage as much as capability that allowed us to make a real difference to our company. The toughest part was deciding to do it. Thanks to all of you for sharing the vision and sharing the load.*

6

Commitment to Change

One way to begin focusing on the quality of your life is by reflecting on such questions as: To what extent do you like the way you are living now? Are there some things in your life that you'd like to change? Do you feel that change is even necessary? It is not a sign of cowardice to have doubts and fears over changing your stance in the world. In fact, it is a mark of bravery to acknowledge your resistance to change and your anxiety over taking increased control. It is a challenge and a struggle to take an honest look at your life and begin to live differently.

Gerald Corey and
Marianne Schneider Corey
I Never Knew I Had a Choice (1993)

The important criterion for any organizational-support function is value-added. The challenge to delight customers has forced companies, quite literally, to strive ruthlessly to reduce waste to the point that every dollar of investment must have an equal or higher worth to customers. Gone are the days of "cushy" budgets, "bench" staff and "time to kill." People are relentless about these changes. It is not a pretty sight!

In fact, the precise reason why this is a problem for many people is that they are involved in considerable activity that involves wasted motion and expense. It is natural for most of us to become defensive about such realities, but at some point we need to stop defending and take a hard look at the truth. Maybe we are contributing exactly the value we intended. If this truth is denied repeatedly, we are sure to be found out in today's business climate. To accept that this may be true, or that with some additional effort, our value contribution could be increased—note that I said accept, not advertise or confess—at least puts us in the position of control . . . which allows us to have a reasonable opportunity to do something about it. Alternatively, rather than admit to any waste, it might be smart to simply challenge ourselves to put some time and effort into improving our performance . . . even if it is already at an acceptable level.

Of course, the problem is not with management—it's all those companies with whom we are competing. Management did not just wake up one day and decide to make life more difficult for Training. This situation is no "cake-walk" for them, you know. They are the ones who have all the "heat" on them. Management is looking to Training to add value simply because the competitive situation requires them to do so. Entire organizations are threatened, and quite possibly, management is threatened more than any other group.

It looks as if Training practitioners have no choice, but in fact it is their decision whether to work in businesses or other economically driven organizations. There are other options out there, and plenty of people that choose them do just fine. But, once the decision is made to get involved in business—today more than ever before—we have to support management when the competitive situation gets intense.

Furthermore, the reason there is so much talk about competitive advantage is that, if a company can establish a competitive advantage, then it will be under less pressure to enforce the value-added rule. If corporate Training—or any other function, for that matter—can move its business to a position of competitive advantage, this alone will ease the pressure on everyone.

PBP is often asked to assess the value-added of a Training function, and other functions, too, and Training has proven to be a controversial function to evaluate. First of all, there is typically very little data to substantiate the impact of Training's work. Number of programs, training days, number of participants – the measures submitted as evidence of Training's contribution – are accurate indicators only of *cost*, not value. Post-course evaluations are often submitted to demonstrate a high level of client satisfaction, and these too are considered insufficient proof. Though evaluations may reflect a favorable immediate response to training activity, they provide no measure of the value created through increased productivity, decreased costs, improved performance, and other measures of value.

Second, there is only sketchy evidence to support the need for ongoing training in most organizations. When "customer needs" surveys are conducted, they are submitted as evidence of need. However, these surveys typically amount to a "wish list" for every kind of course imaginable, usually without any support or justification noted. The only corroborating evidence to suggest a value for this activity is the frequent expression of employees that they personally value the efforts of the Training staff as providers of a way for people to improve themselves.

Make no mistake—there are areas in which training is critical to the operation of a business. Production, distribution, maintenance, and some sales units require training for new employees or related cross-training. Curiously enough, this training is generally provided directly by these units and calls on the Training function only for occasional support.

Ultimately, the Training staff's attempts to solicit explicit client testaments regarding the impact and contribution of specific training programs lead to Training's fate. Many organizations have apparently begun to seriously question the value of Training's activity. Under pressure to justify and probably begin paying for all training that supports their operations, internal clients seem forced to acknowledge that little has really changed as a result of the training received. Furthermore, managers often indicate that training is an impediment to increasing productivity and performance levels. Taking people away from their work for days at a time, and without any noticeable positive difference, simply raises costs.

The subject of adding value, as it relates to Training, is a source of contention for many Training practitioners as well. As a new reality, it is certainly unwanted. As a measure of worth, it is unforgiving. Because Training is a staff support function, it is not easy to calculate value-added in any meaningful way—even when we know that it is there. Our new-found knowledge about "processes" tells us that it is quite often impossible to measure the value-added of any single activity or function involved in any process except the "core" process of a company. The strategic, support and administrative processes involve activities that cannot be broken out piecemeal and evaluated. It is like asking, "What is the value-added of a manager?"

Commitment to Add Greater Value

The example of a Southeastern hospital group may provide us with some additional insight into this issue of value-added. Dr. Jo Benders is director of corporate training for this 15-hospital organization. Dr. Jo, or simply Jo, as most people refer to her, is not a physician, as her title might imply — she is a psychologist. The special thing about Jo is her way with people. She exhibits, probably more than anyone else I have worked with, extraordinary relationship skills. But now that I think about it, Training practitioners as a group all seem to have particularly strong relationship skills. Hmm, maybe there's a connection?

Jo and I met for breakfast on the Tuesday I have in mind, and, for some reason, she was in rare form ready to burst because of the recent turmoil in her mind. She no sooner sat down and signaled the waiter for coffee than she let loose. Fortunately, I took notes, so you can listen in on this turn of events.

"Well, now I understand what has been happening," Jo began. "The rules are changing. It is no longer enough that training activity sounds helpful, regardless of whether it is proposed by management or Training. I guess in the future, training activity will always need to have an impact on the business that will justify the resources expended. Performance, not politics, will be the only acceptable explanation for training. Results, not opinion, will be the measure. What do you think of that?"

I answered by asking, "What's up, Jo?" She barely caught her breath, and continued.

"A radical change for some, perhaps, but a long overdue improvement for this company, if you ask me. All these darn programs — these aren't the intended role of Training, and they don't well utilize the specialized capabilities we have. Then again, it was work, which did let us build up our staff so we can do this kind of quality work in the first place.

"I guess if we plan to work in a competitive business, though, then we will have to play by the new rules. There are other options, you know, if you care to do that kind of stuff. Ultimately, we do have a choice."

"I agree with you, Jo, but we know that many people *don't* think as though they do have a choice. Then they feel trapped, and they start protecting their situation even if it isn't working for them."

"That's right," she continued. "Managers ask us for training to fix their organizational problems, but resist the time and expense it requires because what we do for them never really seems to work anyway. You would think they'd figure it out. When I ask, managers typically estimate that 80 to 90 percent of all training produces no observable change in behavior or performance. Then why do managers consistently turn to training to solve people problems? Great question. In part, because that's the way many of them learned to deal with such concerns, but also because they don't understand enough about human behavior to know that training is rarely the solution. To the manager, if people aren't behaving in a favorable way, then training is prescribed to get someone else involved to hopefully solve the problem. It's not training they want; they just want somebody to fix the darn problem. We just happen to be the only people in the company willing to take on people issues. Managers don't really know a better alternative."

"Why is that, Jo? They're bright people."

"I don't really know, but it may be that *we* are part of the problem."

"We?"

"Oh, sorry. I mean Training is part of the problem. Maybe because training is offered as the antidote to all sorts of individual and organizational ills, the implicit message is that these programs *are* the solution. Need to improve teamwork? No problem—just put everyone through a team-building program. People not talking to each other? It sounds like you need a communications course. Want to increase sales? When was the last time you put the sales force through sales training?

"Training has also become a way for managers to communicate with their organization. A new policy, form or milestone? Give 'em some training. And, talk about the Hawthorne effect. Because training is often seen by organization members as an indication that management has plans for them, we end up being the company reward program. Employees feeling unappreciated? Send them to a course; they deserve some time off."

"More coffee?" I offered. Jo slowed down to 60 words a minute to nod yes. "Sounds like you think the managers are responsible, but Training has contributed to the problem. Is that right?"

"I don't know. What I do know is that we can't blame this situation on managers alone, because Training practitioners have played a big part. When Training is asked to be involved in these situations, we are at once eager to be called on for support and concerned about how to accomplish the impossible task being requested. As a response, we typically ask for as much time and budget as we can *sell* in order to perform the required miracle. We're *forced* to take the offensive to secure the greatest amount of resources possibly available. It's our only hope of influencing the problem situation. I guess we figure that if enough time and effort are expended, just maybe employee performance will improve.

"Unfortunately, time and budget are not the answer, just as training is not the answer. Maybe we can't generalize about what's really called for, but we can generalize that it's probably not training. And the training vendors don't help. Their programs emphasize entertainment to get good 'level ones.' They don't fit the culture very well. The context or specific needs of the situation are never addressed."

"Well, let me ask you, Jo. Do you think it has anything to do with the relationship between managers and Training practitioners? I'm thinking about our discussion about . . . ." I didn't get to finish that sentence.

"Now I see it. Our trainers ask me all the time, 'How do I get management to see the value in training?' From now on I won't give them the self-serving answer they want to hear. My reply needs to be more like, 'Isn't the more important question, how do we get *you* to see the value of management?' Their question is an indication of someone who has gotten so wrapped up in expanding their importance within the organization, they've lost sight of its goals and their reason for being there.

"Our executives are uncertain why they should support training activity, except that employees value it as a symbol of their future potential. Managers ask for it to fix their organizational problems, but resist the time and expense it requires because it never seems to work anyway. Human Resource and Training practitioners promote it for just about everything that ails the organization, yet seem hard pressed to prove its impact and value. What's wrong with this picture?

"All of these are rational perspectives, but they don't really address the principal problem–that training does little to solve the so-called 'people' problems or develop the human-performance opportunities of organizations."

"Put on your psychologist hat for a minute, Jo. Be your own counseling client for a minute. Think about it in that context."

"Okay. What do you do at that point when you have tried the well-established approach, time after time, and it has not worked? Do you try again even one more time, or is this simply throwing good money after bad? Do you start over, this time taking a radically new, even counter-intuitive approach? Or do you simply cut your losses and assume that no solution exists? Living with the frustration, at some point, becomes worse than being unproductive. It's mind-numbing.

Resources are wasted trying to fix what doesn't seem fixable. I need a life."

"We all do. Why don't we talk about something else?"

"I can't, Jim. This whole training thing is a mess. Maybe the execs ought to pull the plug on Training. I've read enough stories about departments being downsized or even eliminated. Maybe that's the kind of bold gesture it will take to effect the needed changes in how training activity is conducted in this organization. Traditional training programs are such an accepted part of our organizational culture. Subtle efforts to change them will surely be resisted throughout the organization — simply to maintain the status quo.

"It's not a capricious strategy. Abandonment is the first step in a turnaround. If the current arrangement doesn't work, or cannot be made to work, then it goes. You have to get rid of what's not working first, so as to free up resources for something that might. Sure, we naturally resist abandoning anything, even the obsolete, the plans that didn't work, and the plans that once worked but now don't. But this feeling passes. After six months or so, we'll probably wonder why it took so long to take action. Maybe I need to tell them we quit. Well, I can't do that. Maybe I need to quit. No, that won't accomplish anything. I'm probably one of the few in our department who have begun to catch on. If I quit, this will just continue. No, what I need to do is stay and fix it. That's it. I need to set the course for the future of how Training will operate in this company. That's what I'm going to do. I guess that's why I called you."

"It sounds as though the situation won't change until *somebody* does something to set the course. And you're particularly well respected in the company. But you might want to sleep on a big decision like that one before you make it public information. So how can I help?"

"Well, tell me. What can I do? Where do I start? When I think back to your workshop, I keep coming up with things to do, but no real strategy that fits this special situation. All I can think of is: don't train . . . solve problems; training is never the complete solution; training *may* be an important part of the solution; don't train without management support of the instruction; design learning into work processes; minimize classroom training time and costs; train for results, and nothing less; train just in time, on the job, and organization-wide; facilitate self-directed learning; provide training interventions that achieve dramatic improvements in learning, in effectiveness, and in the new business measures of performance . . . quality, speed, cost, flexibility and innovation . . . for *our* clients.

"Which leads me to the conclusion that we desperately need a fundamental rethinking of how we approach training. Jim, that's what *you* said."

"Yes, I did say that. But more important now is the fact that *you've* said it, and said it in such a way that I believe you mean it."

"I do mean it. When can we get started?"

"We already have."

Time for New Thinking

Organization members need to strive for greater value-added so they can enjoy the benefits associated with working with a successful enterprise. The real pressure for value-added is a self-imposed pressure for self-betterment—the desire to do what is right and what is beneficial— for ourselves, for our fellow organization members, and for the enterprise all of us serve.

The pursuit of value-added is an opportunity more than it is a problem to be solved. This realization does not reduce the challenge, but it does provide the motivation.

Part III

Performance and Productivity

We live in a world that is becoming increasingly complex.
Unfortunately, our styles of thinking rarely match this complexity.
We often end up persuading ourselves that everything is more simple
than it actually is, dealing with complexity by presuming that
it does not really exist. This is very evident in the way fad and fashion
dominate approaches to organizational analysis and problem-solving,
an interest in one type of solution or set of techniques quickly giving way
to another.

Gareth Morgan
Images of Organization (1986)

With the publishing of Drucker's *The Practice of Management* in 1954, management emerged as a *discipline*—a formal methodology on the means to obtain economic results—to deal with new and more-complex challenges that accompanied the almost boundless expansion of business organizations following World War II. Previously, business owners and managers had crafted their actions from the principles asserted by Fayol, Taylor and Weber in the early twentieth century for designing work and organizations. These same principles then proliferated in the military and in civilian industry during World War II, establishing the "machine bureaucracy" as the accepted design for structuring, operating and managing organizations.

Machine and electronic technologies and financial strength were seen as the critical competitive resources, whereas people were relegated to a role of adapting to support a company's chosen technology. *Performance*—the *effective* satisfaction of customer needs—was designed into machine processes and standard procedures, and not generally subject to human skill. *Productivity*—the *efficient* application of human effort—was achieved through work redesign and computer automation. *Training*—formal instruction to direct, correct and *standardize* in workers the proper skills, knowledge and attitude to perform their work—played an important role in organizations as a tool for the bureaucratization of work processes and human behavior.

The New Work of Management

Since then, the challenge of management has undergone considerable change. The emergence of global markets and competitors, information and communications technology, and very large-scale organizations of well-educated and sophisticated employees, along with the increasingly refined discipline of management, has added significantly to the complexity of management practice. In contrast to its early focus on the strategically planned achievement of objectives utilizing capital, labor and natural resources, management is better characterized today as

> *the systemic and purposeful application of specialized knowledge resources for maximum attainable performance and productivity* (Drucker, 1993).

Today, knowledge is the key economic resource; capital, labor and natural resources have become secondary, and can be obtained easily with knowledge and ingenuity. Not just any knowledge, but specialized and advanced knowledge capable of producing economic results . . . knowledge that proves its worth in performance.

Accordingly, organizations have acquired new structure, new systems and new importance to management. Advancements in the technologies and practices for most kinds of work have led to the development of organizations that now consist mostly of specialists—individuals who know more about their own specialty than anyone else in the organization does. Even factory workers, particularly in highly automated production operations, increasingly have more knowledge of their work than their supervisors do. The organization can no longer be thought of simply as "labor" required to do the work designed and directed by management; the organization has become management's source of knowledge and principal transformer of knowledge into value for customers. Because of this shift, organizations must now be managed on the basis of *responsibility* rather than "command and control." Drucker arrives at this same conclusion in *Post-Capitalist Society* (1993) and elaborates on the consequences for management:

The knowledge-based organization therefore requires that everyone take responsibility for that organization's objectives, contribution, and, indeed, for its behavior as well.

This implies that all members of the organization must think through their objectives and their contributions, and then take responsibility for both. It implies that there are no "subordinates"; there are only "associates." Furthermore, in the knowledge-based organization all members have to be able to control their own work by feedback from their results to their objectives. All members must ask themselves: "What is the one major contribution to this organization and its mission which I can make at this particular time?" It requires, in other words, that all members act as responsible decision makers. All members have to see themselves as "executives."

If managers are to manage knowledge-based organizations, the practice of management must advance dramatically. Management's challenge is to unlearn its traditional "command and control" methods that were appropriate for the unskilled and semi-skilled work of "machine bureaucracies," in which knowledge was centralized in a few top executives. To manage effectively, management must learn how to successfully *facilitate* and *support* the achievement of maximum performance and productivity by every responsibility-driven individual and group within the organization. This is the *new work* of management.

Traditionally, to deal with people issues, senior management has deflected this work to layers of supervision and to staff functions, such as Industrial Relations, Human Resources and Training. By applying Taylor's scientific management principles to labor—redesigning manual tasks so they could be learned and performed efficiently by unskilled workers—U.S. industry has successfully improved the performance and productivity of this shrinking segment of the workforce. Not so for knowledge workers and service workers—with these workers, work-design principles have yielded only marginal gains in performance and have proven ineffective in increasing productivity.

Since the 1950s, repeated attempts to directly improve human performance and increase productivity have invariably taken on the character of social goals and have been limited to concerns usually portrayed as *human relations*. Generally taking the form of mandated, large-scale education and training programs, these attempts have been implemented piecemeal as presumed-helpful knowledge emerged—earning the sarcastic label, *program of the month*. In the minds of organization members, such attempts lacked substance because they were directed from a source other than management itself and offered no substantial changes in fundamental practices. Many of these efforts amounted to little more that psychological manipulation, and given their transparency, contributed to employees' increasing skepticism, if not cynicism, about management. Worse yet, the challenge to improve white-collar performance and productivity has gone unmet.

Human Performance and Productivity

Today, *knowledge* is the critical resource and *people* are the source of value. With their unique capacity to perceive, reason and make judgments, people provide companies with the means to generate, retain and apply knowledge—people provide the capability to acquire and convert knowledge resources to value, and to innovate and substitute when specific knowledge is unavailable or insufficient. Capitalizing on this potential throughout the past 50 years, companies have progressively standardized, systematized, and automated production operations to increase productivity—converting unskilled and semi-skilled manual work into skilled technician work, and advancing labor roles to knowledge and service specialist roles, where they add greater value. Only recently has management begun to tap this same potential in technical, administrative and service operations. Increasing the performance and productivity of these specialists is the central challenge facing management.

Management can no longer afford to think of people simply as labor with which to operate a machine, staff a process or perform a simple task; to be effective, management must rethink its approach to managing people and, in particular, must recognize the importance, discretionary nature and greater potential for performance of knowledge and service specialists, who generate and apply knowledge for results. Today, with more than 80 percent of the workforce utilized in these *professional roles*, people have become the direct source of customer value . . . and the source of competitive advantage as well.

Making improvements in the performance and productivity of salespeople, engineers, nurses, service technicians, machine operators, administrative specialists, and others will not be easy and will require radical changes in the structure and systems of organizations. Management must lead and support these changes, and though it is in employees' best interests to support such initiatives, management can expect many employees to resist these changes simply to preserve that which is familiar. To be successful, management will need to enlist the support of well-liked executives, informal leaders and savvy support staffers like Training practitioners to facilitate these initiatives.

If successful, this effort will result in a more supportive and democratic workplace, and with it a new premise for employee opportunity that more equitably rewards people who have invested and who continue to invest in advanced education, the acquisition of advanced skills, and higher levels of human development—all of which advance employees' capacity to add value in their work. Since employee performance and productivity create the earnings from which wages are paid, and people can be paid only in accordance with their value-added, then removing the performance and productivity barriers indigenous to today's largely bureaucratic workplace will result in personal financial gain for knowledge and service specialists.

In cases where the initiatives to radically restructure and change organizations fail, the future is much less certain. There is clear evidence from the past several years that competitive industries and markets will not allow such organizations to survive.

Emphasis on Knowledge

Since the early 1970s, we have witnessed an unparalleled expansion of technological development, including information, communication and transportation technology. These advances have transformed a world of parochial economies into an inextricably linked *global economy* of global markets and global competition. New rules for corporate survival and competitive advantage emerged from this transformation, not the least of which was the requirement to continuously improve the quality of every aspect of work. Consequently, advancing technology fueled new performance requirements, along with new tools and more sophisticated methods with which to meet these requirements. These developments have increased the need for specialization and requisite knowledge for every organization function. Today, because managers can no longer know how to perform the jobs of their subordinates or be there to witness and control their behavior, it is necessary for organization members to exercise greater responsibility for their work and its value contribution to the enterprise.

Among their responsibilities, knowledge and service specialists must govern what they know and do not know. They also must govern what they need to know and do not need to know. Management cannot possibly make these determinations for specialists; management can only be clear in its expectations regarding performance and productivity so specialists can ascertain their own needs. Whatever specialists do not know but need to know, they must be responsible for learning. Furthermore, they must also know what knowledge and services they can procure from others, and they need to work effectively across all boundaries, inside and outside the formal organization, to access the knowledge and other resources they require to carry out their responsibilities. Once again, management cannot govern these actions. Consistent with their responsibilities, these workers must bring together the requisite knowledge and service to create value.

As introduced in Chapter 2 and further discussed in Chapter 10, high-performance work systems (HPWS) must be structured around knowledge—particularly its acquisition, maintenance, application and generation—to support the innumerable knowledge and service specialists in today's organizations. These organizations are flat in comparison to political hierarchies and are focused on business processes rather than on functions so as to maximize the flow and speed of knowledge transferred between specialists. The goals of the organization—goals that clearly state objectives and expectations for all specialists—provide needed structure. And, with well-organized feedback, each organization member can exercise self-management by comparing outcomes with expectations. Management's role is necessarily redefined as providing needed *leadership* and *support*.

To maintain their competency, specialists must be persistently concerned with learning in four areas, focusing both on their specialist capabilities and challenges, and on the objectives, practices and immediate concerns of the enterprise at large:

1. *All relevant technologies*
   Fluency must be maintained in all relevant technologies and sciences, in addition to the specialists' own disciplines. Having a discerning level of understanding in other areas of knowledge facilitates cross-functional dialogue and collaboration.

2. *Significant practice skills*
   Mastery is essential in work methods and in the application of technology in order to perform high-quality work. Competent specialists must have consummate professional skills and self-discipline.

3. *Assessment of current reality*

Acumen in assessing all information—feedback in particular—requires a broad understanding of the external environment and organizational context of any assignment. Keen insight, with accuracy and quickness of judgment, is a high priority for specialists.

4. *Creation of new knowledge*

Proficiency in creating new knowledge requires specialists to solve problems and develop opportunities through innovative and enterprising action. Going beyond the acquisition of existing knowledge, they need to practice behaviors that facilitate *learning*[2]—the creation of new knowledge.*

In addition to this extensive requirement for knowledge pertaining to their functional work, specialists will also be accountable for increasingly higher levels of competency in the core work methods of the firm(s) they serve, the level of authority they hold and the exact role they serve. These methods could readily include specific best-practice behaviors for communicating, decision-making and teamwork—behaviors taken for granted yet practiced widely and relied on for highly effective and efficient interpersonal work.

Management's Challenge

Support for workplace learning[2] is management's responsibility; however, management now relies too fully for its accomplishment on the capabilities of Training practitioners. Adults learn[2] most when they are

---

* Because of Peter Senge's extensive and purposeful use of the word *learning* when speaking of "the creation of new knowledge" in *The Fifth Discipline*, it has become necessary to distinguish between the two definitions, or distinctly different kinds, of learning: (1) "acquiring existing knowledge," which is the meaning Training practitioners traditionally attribute to the word *learning*, and (2) "creating new knowledge," which is Senge's *only* meaning for the word *learning* (Senge, 1990, pp. 13-14). To ensure clarity when I use the word *learning*, I refer to Senge's use of the word as *learning*[2], assigning the symbol "2" to indicate the required "double loop" of cognition required to create new knowledge. In the first attempt at cognition (i.e., first loop) one acquires only existing knowledge. Then in a second attempt at cognition (i.e., second loop) one reflects on this acquired knowledge to determine its meaning, significance, limitations, etc., thus creating new knowledge—*learning*[2] (Argyris, 1982).

performing, facing challenges and achieving objectives. Classroom activities can be helpful, but only if they closely resemble the actual work situation and there is support on the job to transfer what is learned in class into full capability at work. The workplace learning[2] challenge requires more extensive and effective resources than are provided to Training practitioners. Moreover, managers and unschooled Training practitioners err when they equate learning[2] with training, as they are vastly different. Training is an attempt to control . . . to standardize . . . to show people the approved way to do their work. Learning is the goal of training, yet *substantial learning* — beyond awareness — requires (1) purpose, (2) study, (3) practice, (4) adaptation and (5) integration with current knowledge and behavior. Progressing further, learning[2] begins *only* after the acquisition of existing knowledge, skills and attitudes (i.e., cognitive, psychomotor and affective content that resides in others), and necessarily extends to the creation of completely new knowledge, methods and perspectives as people understand, apply and adapt new subject matter to their circumstances. Learning[2] is an individual, self-directed activity associated with developing, changing and growing. Management will need to provide for training, learning and learning[2] for its people, and it will need to understand the difference to get what it wants.

Though many organizations make a significant investment in training, the support provided by this investment does little to meet the learning and learning[2] needs of employees. Corporate training activity is frequently limited to formal classroom programs that attempt to standardize basic knowledge and practices, and is further limited to basic-level instruction — hardly sufficient in breadth or depth to support specialists working in diverse disciplines to achieve higher levels of performance. This is not to say that the current level of investment is necessarily too low, just that it is not used for support initiatives that are truly helpful. It is not uncommon for an objective assessment of training activity to uncover the fact that 50 to 90 percent of the current investment in formal training programs yields very little or no value. Worse yet, the organization's learning and learning[2] needs go unmet.

To the objective reader, such an outcome is not surprising, since workplace training was conceived as an intervention at the turn of the century to standardize the work of unskilled and semi-skilled workers. Workplace training was, and still can be, a very successful method for organizations to support the standardization of work processes, outputs, skills and norms for the purpose of achieving coordination within a hierarchy, such as in government services, regulated industries, high-risk situations, etc. Also, training is a key design parameter in all work considered "professional," such as accounting, medicine, pharmacy, law, etc. Notwithstanding this appropriate use of training, there are many employee learning needs, even in bureaucracies, that cannot be satisfied with current training methods.

Since the 1950s, many organizations, or parts of them, have gradually moved away from a purely bureaucratic design. Companies in all industries that formed since World War II have started with alternative structures. In these less-bureaucratic organizations, training is much less effective even when used for its original purpose—as a tool for standardization—because standardization is less acceptable and appropriate in the post-industrial organization. Training is also less effective in organizations consisting largely of knowledge and service specialists, and in organizations moving toward the HPWS concept. Furthermore, standardization is somewhat incompatible in companies which emphasize diversity, empowerment, high involvement, responsibility for quality at the source, teamwork, self-direction and other organizational characteristics that imply individual responsibility, discretion and initiative-taking. This is no surprise to executives who have undoubtedly failed in any effort to train empowerment, quality or participation into existence in their organizations. Moreover, training is an ineffective tool for adult development. Other intervention methods have proven themselves to be more effective in these settings.

Knowledge and service specialists—the "professionals" of today's organizations—are responsive to standardization as it is required by their professions and their professions' work processes, outputs, skills and norms . . . but much less responsive to any unwanted standardization attempted by an organization. One of the characteristics that make these specialists "professional" is their acceptance of responsibility for their own knowledge, skills, performance and learning needs. Accordingly, it is not practical for an organization to provide training that goes beyond support for elements of work and behavior that are appropriate and strongly desired by a large segment of the organization. Since most of the work in organizations today is professional or almost professional—each specialty having its own technology and practice skills and requiring the standardization of certain work processes, outputs, skills and norms—companies must find more effective and efficient alternatives than training to better satisfy the extensive learning and performance-improvement needs of organization members.

The most important knowledge that management needs to acquire and capitalize on today is how to create and maintain an HPWS that maximizes the performance of people in converting knowledge to value. Once such knowledge is obtained, then management will be prepared to reconsider the learning[2], performance and productivity support requirements of its organizations.

Humaneering

In Part III, I introduce the reader to a concept that I developed for a client in 1989 to teach its executives and managers a very practical approach for integrating the many theories and models advanced during the past 50 years regarding human behavior, learning, performance and productivity at work. In particular, it enabled them to determine appropriate support for their organization, including the effective *and expanded* utilization of staff professionals . . . like Training. Since then, I have shared this concept with additional clients also faced with this problem . . . each time finding that it successfully resolves long-standing confusion that has kept management from taking effective action.

One aspect of this concept is a process model that emphasizes the principal issues management needs to understand, and the organizational support that will be required, in order to realize the significant value contribution inherent in a company's organization. It portrays a *vital linkage* that integrates, advances and also simplifies what we now know about human behavior, learning, performance and productivity in the workplace. Because it outlines this challenge with new clarity, it has proven to be a helpful tool for senior executives, managers, and first-line supervisors, as well as for Human Resources and Training directors and practitioners. At once, it offers a more comprehensive alternative to models that focus on only one or a few aspects of learning, performance *or* productivity, and it better represents the true complexity of these goals in easy-to-understand terms.

Chapter 7, "Vital Linkage," introduces the concept of "Humaneering" and outlines the *Humaneering process algorithm*, providing an overview of its six integrated stages, on which the four subsequent chapters elaborate. Chapters 8-11 present the final four stages in reverse order — the order in which the stages must be implemented — starting with the end point or goal of *organizational competitive advantage*, and detailing the principal issues and activities involved in the transformation that occurs in each phase of the process. Chapter 8, "Humaneering for Advantage," discusses the importance of having a *corporate strategy* for organizational competitive advantage in order to maximize learning, performance and productivity.   Chapter 9, "Innovation for Productivity," considers the requirements and methods for continually increasing organizational *productivity* by influencing the work environment. Chapter 10, "Working for Performance," discusses the transformation from human capability to human performance, now an important concern of Training due to its recent progress in making *performance* the objective of its work. Chapter 11, "Studying for Competence," concludes Part III with a discussion of effective and efficient methods for preparing employees for their work, as well as a strategy for raising *employee competence*.

7

Vital Linkage

If we are to make sense of human performance, it will be because we develop simple and useful vantage points when we discuss it . . . . we must have a way to sort out our viewpoints and weigh our values if we are going to communicate.

Thomas F. Gilbert
Human Competence (1978)

Since management emerged as a discipline in the mid-1950s, we have witnessed a virtual explosion of new information and theories regarding every feature of a contemporary business. Much of this new thinking has been in response to the seemingly ever-increasing organizational challenges management is having to face, and more recently to the recognition that the effectiveness of a company's human capital may soon be the final frontier for establishing a sustainable competitive advantage. This abundance of information has been followed by a rapid expansion of support staffs, whose role it is to compile, interpret and apply this knowledge.

Management Needs Support

Since I make a living in part by keeping up with business- and management-related research and writing, I naturally value the data, insights and models that are offered. However, that can hardly be the case for any executive, line manager or even the director of a staff function. Most business functions have become very complex and sophisticated; the work being done by almost everyone in an organization has its own technology, methodology, emerging theories, research, etc.

Even if line managers and staff directors wanted to keep up, and even if they could devote a sizable part of their day to the task, they still could not do so without help. Let me confess that the only way I can keep up is to rely on the support of research assistants who gather the product of this knowledge explosion and review it with me. Though this kind of service should be a responsibility of the support functions in most organizations, bureaucratic turf battles have in many cases produced sufficient myopia and self-promotion that these staffs are no longer useful in this way.

Executives, managers and directors need help if they are to benefit from the significant developments during the past 50 years in the fields of human behavior, learning, performance and productivity, as they apply to the workplace. Only recently has the organization as an entity become a substantial topic in the top MBA programs, so we can imagine that most executives and managers have little basis on which to incorporate new developments as they occur. All too often, they feel forced to rely solely on personal experience for their understanding of how best to accomplish their organizational objectives . . . and although this is a certainly a valuable starting point, it hardly taps the sophisticated understanding we now have about when, where, why and how people work the way they do. As a result, many businesspeople with significant responsibility for and impact on the course of their organizations are compelled to make important people-related decisions—decisions that will have an extraordinary effect on the capability and effectiveness of individuals, groups and even entire organizations—without a firm grasp of their alternatives and of the probable consequences of those alternatives. A fitting example is management's current over-reliance on training to deal with almost every conceivable people-related issue in an organization—the *"throw training at the problem"* solution. Routinely, the consequences of this approach include higher-than-necessary expenses, lost productivity, unresolved issues, a demotivated workforce, and persistent barriers to high performance. Such waste is becoming intolerable. Increasingly, management has to find some way to obtain this knowledge so that it can effectively and efficiently support its organizations' requirements for enhancements to learning, performance and productivity.

Humaneering

Though management has been plagued by the lack of this important knowledge for at least as long as I have been working in industry— since 1969—it was not until 20 years later that I was first retained to address this problem. One aspect of my response that has persisted because of its apparent helpfulness to executives and managers is the concept of *Humaneering*. PBP's intervention included a series of client-sponsored management conferences on performance improvement, titled "Humaneering: Human Performance Technology at Work," at which we taught an integration of more than 100 scientific laws, theories and models concerning human behavior, technology transfer, organizational learning[2], performance improvement, organizational productivity, managed change and related concerns to 3,000 executives and managers. *Humaneering* is a word blend that I originally coined for this client engagement; however, subsequent client interest in Humaneering's integrated framework has begun to institutionalize use of the word for a growing number of people. I introduce the Humaneering framework here because it provides a helpful context for examining Training's past activity and recommending changes that will increase Training's value-added.

Humaneering is at the heart of an admittedly bold yet very practical idea—integrating into a *new* applied science our abundant knowledge pertaining to workplace learning, performance and productivity. (See **Figure 7.1**.) Currently, it is a formidable task for businesspeople to access this knowledge because it is found dispersed throughout many branches of science, practice disciplines and fields of inquiry. Furthermore, this integration would for some resolve the mistaken perception that such knowledge is mutually exclusive—that theories must compete because only one theory can be accurate—and would substantiate the fact that all of these scientific laws, supported theories and substantiated models are in fact valid and complementary explanations of human nature, perhaps dependent only on certain circumstances for their predicted or described effect to be demonstrated. The act itself of exposing executives and managers to Humaneering— suggesting that they think of it as an integrated applied science that focuses on maximizing human achievement at work—precipitates a dramatic shift in how they view employees; in how they view learning, performance and productivity; and in how they work to support their human capital.

Figure 7.1
Organization of the numerous branches of empirical science, indicating the proper placement of *humaneering* among the applied sciences.
(adapted from a similar chart in Strahler, 1992)

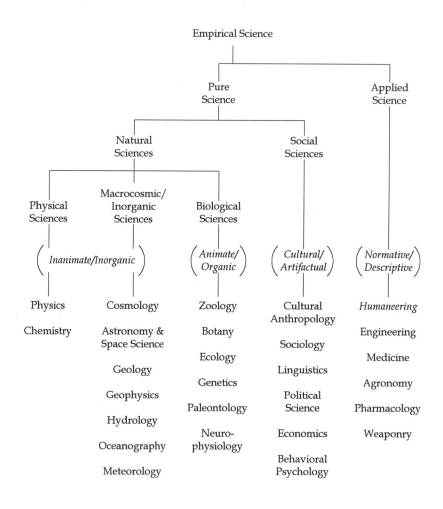

Formally, I define *Humaneering* as "the application of scientific principles concerning human beings to practical ends, such as the operation of effective organizations." Humaneering corresponds to engineering—

> *the application of mathematical and scientific principles to practical ends, as the design, construction, and operation of economical and efficient structures, equipment and (mechanical) systems* (Soukhanov, 1988)

—except that engineering implies the application of science to *physical* and *mechanical* contrivances, whereas Humaneering focuses on *human beings*. Humaneering is also distinguished from human engineering—

> *the industrial management of labor; the technology of the efficient use of machines by human beings* (Soukhanov, 1988)

—because the focus of human engineering, as in engineering, is on machines and their optimization, with reference to human beings only as the users of machines. The focus of Humaneering is on human beings and their optimization, making reference to machines, technology and other elements of the work setting only to support and extend human potential.

The emergence of a Humaneering science is at some point inevitable following the extraordinary evolution of knowledge about the enhancement of human capability as it relates to learning, performance and productivity at work. Science is, after all, the acquisition, classification, and analysis of reliable (i.e., based on observation and experience) knowledge of the real world (Strahler, 1992). According to science philosopher Ernest Nagel, "It is the desire for explanations that are at once systematic and controllable by factual evidence that generates science" (1961). To executives and managers, it is the ability to see the order that exists amidst the visible chaos of organizations.

A significant effort was made by the National Society of Performance and Instruction (NSPI) in its preparation of a comprehensive *Handbook of Human Performance Technology*, published by Jossey-Bass, Inc., in 1992. (As a testament to the quality of this text, we give each participant a copy at several of our workshops.) This work integrates much of the thinking and methods from the fields of instruction and organization development in an effort to adapt the field of education . . . NSPI's roots . . . to the workplace requirement for economic results.

Figure 7.2
The Humaneering Process for Developing Organizational Competitive Advantage

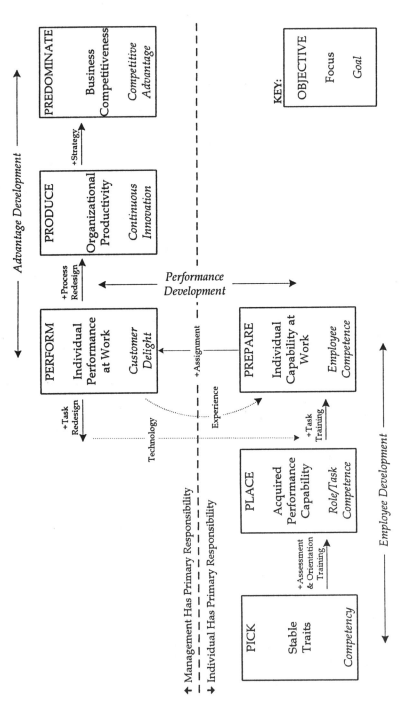

Humaneering incorporates the same fields as human perform-ance technology, yet extends beyond them to tap both scientific and practice knowledge from fields as diverse as corporate strategy, work design, organization design, organization behavior, compensation, management science, industrial engineering, industrial management, management accounting, finance, economics, environmental science, cybernetics, ergonomics, communications, anthropology, sociology, psychology and medicine. Furthermore, the inclusive philosophical basis of Humaneering seeks to distinguish fundamental theories, not by whether one theory is right and another is wrong, but by viewing all well-substantiated theories as valid under certain circumstances . . . and Humaneering attempts to define these conditions based on the re-search upon which a theory is materially based. The remaining chal-lenge for executives and managers in applying Humaneering science is to ascertain a factual understanding of their organizations' prevailing circumstances and to determine their objectives.

The Humaneering Process

In addition to identifying this integrated applied science, the word *Hu-maneering* also describes the use of this knowledge — *the Humaneering process* — in the form of a six-stage algorithm concerned primarily with the challenge to advance human achievement to the highest possible level through systematically focusing on the support that is required at each stage of the process. (See **Figure 7.2**.) This *process algorithm* helps managers make sense of their organizational challenges, aids them in sorting out the many emerging theories and concepts for addressing these challenges, and guides them in determining the most appropriate role for the many staff-support functions — all for the purpose of maximizing the human resource contribution to an enterprise. It clari-fies and very neatly integrates this formidable task, putting each indi-vidual challenge in its proper sequence.

This chapter focuses on the *vital linkage* that is represented in the Humaneering process algorithm, whereas the four subsequent chapters will examine in greater detail the last four elements of the process, referred to as PREPARE, PERFORM, PRODUCE and PREDOMINATE. The first two elements in the process, though no less important than any one of the other elements, receive less emphasis in this book because the corporate Training function has a more limited involvement in selection and placement (i.e., PICK and PLACE). The quality of recruiting and placement efforts does have a considerable impact on the potential for the balance of the development process, and I do not intend for my emphasis to suggest otherwise.

There are six distinct *stages* in the Humaneering process algorithm, each of which is referred to in terms of an *objective*. Each stage also indicates the principal *focus* and *goal* relating to this objective. The first three objectives comprise the *employee development phase*, for which each individual employee has primary responsibility. The second group of three objectives comprises the *advantage development phase*, for which management has primary responsibility. These two phases are linked by the *performance development phase*, for which employees, management and corporate Training share responsibility. Between the objectives, the *fundamental interventions* are noted, preceded by a "+" sign to show their addition to the process algorithm.

The line separating the *employee development* and *advantage development* phases of the Humaneering process algorithm is significant because as individuals take *assignments*, their efforts need to shift from *self-development* to *performance development*. At this point, they begin to serve the enterprise actively, and management then has primary responsibility for their contributions to the enterprise. Though the employees' principal goal in *performance development* is to increase customer satisfaction in any way appropriate for their role, there are also two byproducts of this effort. First, *technology* is developed, which is integrated into *task training* for subsequent newcomers. Second, employees gain *experience*, which adds to their *employee competence*.

The central point to be made in regard to using the Humaneering process algorithm is that—in the course of fully capitalizing on the human component of an enterprise—learning, performance and productivity are not synonymous, they are not stimulated and supported with the same interventions, they do not occur without directed effort, and they are not achieved simply as a result of training. Training has a role to play in this complex process, but training activity is neither the only nor the principal intervention required. In some situations, training can be detrimental—adding to the difficulty in and unlikelihood of achieving the objective, while slowing the process, raising costs and lowering productivity. So as to not single out Training in making this point, it can be said that the same potential irrelevance and harm are possible for other support-staff functions and their interventions as well.

Chapters 8-11 further explain how to achieve the objectives of the last four stages of the process algorithm (PREPARE, PERFORM,

PRODUCE and PREDOMINATE). But before focusing on any part of the process in detail, the reader might be helped by following an informal "tour" of the process algorithm from left to right—as it might be experienced by an individual employee moving through each objective—to demonstrate the interrelatedness of the elements. Keep in mind, however, that the *design and implementation* of Humaneering take the reverse order, with each element establishing a context and objective for the element directly preceding it in the algorithm. Chapters 8-11 follow this design and implementation order.

Imagine an employee, perhaps yourself, moving through the context of each element of the Humaneering process:

1. **PICK**
    The first objective is to *select the right kind of people* for the organization.

    -   *Define the culture and environment.*
        The challenge begins with determining what personal characteristics, or *stable traits*, the company seeks, both overall and with regard to specific roles to be filled. The goal should be to identify the characteristics (competencies) of people who will perform particularly well.

    -   *Hire the people, not their skills.*
        Then, depending on the existing market for employees, the company will make either an aggressive or a passive recruiting effort to communicate these needs and desires so as to attract people with the best fit of competencies and work-related capabilities for the organization's culture and work. Emphasis should be placed on finding people who are a good fit with the organization, with less concern placed on the skills and experience required to perform specific work functions that can be learned. Capable people can learn the work. People who are not a good fit for the organization will be disruptive and will perform poorly. When recruiting for professional roles, the implicit assumption is that all candidates have the requisite professional skills and experience, or they would not receive consideration in the first place.

- *Make applicants responsible.*
  The company should utilize a variety of methods to assess and screen applicants. At some point, however, the responsibility for excellent selection should shift to the applicants themselves, who must decide whether the organization is one for which they can perform sufficiently well to meet management's expectations, while simultaneously meeting their own needs and desires for the position. They have, or should have, as much or more at risk than the company.

- *Enhance company briefings.*
  Within this objective, there is only limited activity now appropriate for the corporate Training function. Training might provide information briefings about the organization to applicants . . . perhaps doing so in an experiential way so that candidates really understand what the company is like.

2. **PLACE**
   The second objective is to *situate people* in required roles within the organization. The way this is done is critical to employees' success, and decisive in the value to be received by companies.

- *Introduce the organization.*
  Assuming that organizations do select people first for their competencies, the next step is to conduct further *assessment and orientation-training* activities appropriate to fully introduce employees to the organization, indoctrinate them to the way it works, and then familiarize them with the work options for which they are best suited. Only when employees are brought into organizations with an effective introduction can they serve companies with their full human potential to meet the organizations' needs.

- *Enhance orientation training.*
  Although Training might end up with the challenge of working with underqualified or incapable new employees when it comes time to prepare them to work, there is only a minimal defined role for corporate Training at this stage of the process. However, since much of the orientation

training offered by companies is judged by new employees to be ineffective and largely worthless, perhaps the corporate Training function should seize the opportunity to develop an exceptional program that truly meets the needs ɔf both new employees and management.

3. **PREPARE**
   The third objective in the Humaneering process is to *prepare newly placed employees* sufficiently for them to meet the performance specifications of their new roles.

   - *Learn the organization and the role.*
     Once new or existing employees are officially placed in roles, it is essential for them (1) to meet members of their new organizational unit—that is, if the new employees have not already been interviewed and even selected by them, and (2) to learn the current technology, methods, procedures, systems, etc., regarding the role to be assumed. Whatever level of *employee competence* these people may have reached elsewhere, they will be required to learn through instruction, study and experience and to adapt appropriately to demonstrate similar or increased competence in their new positions.

   - *Obtain necessary task training.*
     The focus of effective task training is to increase workers' role or task capability, bringing them up to a minimum acceptable standard of performance. Even professionals, who practice their profession using many of the same methods and procedures regardless of where they work, need to learn the unique characteristics of the work performed in the selected organization. Often this standardization is provided in the form of structured learning of some kind, yet sometimes it is left up to the employees to learn for themselves on the job, with or without helpful coaching. This effort is to make the employees' work consistent with the work required by management and performed by others in a similar role . . . to the extent that standardization is desirable in the role being assumed.

- *Learn the newest technology.*
  It is important for this type of *task training* to reflect the reality of the way work is really performed *in the field* or *on the floor*. Misalignment occurs when work-design changes have been made to the work as it is actually performed, yet this new *technology* is not reflected in up-to-date task training.

- *Avoid general development training.*
  Note that there is no provision for general development training in this *employee development* phase of the Humaneering process. Though more will be said in subsequent chapters about training that may be appropriate *for performance development*, PBP's research indicates that the impact of general development training is very limited and isolated, and therefore relatively meaningless to employers—*a poor investment*. For training to have value in the workplace, it must provide instruction in knowledge, skills and behavior that are required for specific work assignments or that are standard for all work within the organization. This is task training, a key ingredient of this stage in the Humaneering process.

4. **PERFORM**
   The fourth objective is to bring people with new roles quickly up to required performance levels. The focus in the Humaneering process now shifts from *employee development* to *advantage development*, and the immediate goal is *customer satisfaction*. Management is charged with the responsibility of accomplishing this work.

- *Achieve peak performance.*
  Assuming that employees have learned the basic tasks, processes and systems that are involved in their work, the goal of employees is to do whatever they can to help management accomplish the work. Maximum *individual performance at work* is the goal. For Training to contribute to meaningful employee development once employees are at work, it has to provide performance-development support—self-instruction, training, problem-solving or internal consulting—that is on target, just enough, and just in time

to improve their performance. Learning that is integrated into the work, perhaps in the form of performance support systems, is the best option. Once employees are at work, traditional classroom training only disrupts performance, reduces productivity and capacity, and frustrates employees and their managers, who are accountable for performance. Yet rarely is the content transferred effectively to the sites where the work is performed.

- *Provide a supportive environment.*
  It is critical at this stage that employees be completely focused on the task at hand. Employees otherwise focused on themselves and not on their work — commonly the result of not feeling satisfied in the treatment they are receiving from the company — tend to do the minimum and to become inflexible. Have you ever thought or heard the statement, "If the company doesn't care, then I sure won't"? Characteristically, dissatisfied people will fail to champion or support change that improves performance.

- *Make continuous improvements.*
  Furthermore, the product or service that satisfies customers in today's marketplace will be insufficient for tomorrow's. This constant need to improve presents an even greater challenge than achieving customer satisfaction today. A continuous process of task redesign is required to improve performance in terms of the quality, speed, cost, flexibility and innovation of the work output. TQM initiatives are focused on this challenge.

- *Cross-train for skill versatility.*
  To achieve flexibility in adjusting to changes in the business environment, a company must be able to redeploy its employees at will. To facilitate this process, employees should first possess all of the skills within their own skill groups and then diversify to learn the crafts involved in the other positions in their units of the organization. They should have hands-on experience in all assignments.

- *Update task training.*
  Improvements in the form of new "technology" should then be integrated into the task training received by future newcomers to this work.

- *Enhance employee competence.*
  Moreover, as employees perform their work, they also gain valuable experience that adds to their overall competence.

5. **PRODUCE**
The fifth objective is to *increase productivity* while maintaining or improving performance.   Customer satisfaction is not enough.

- *Increase productivity.*
  A fundamental law of the marketplace is that a company's *organizational productivity* — its output per unit of human effort (e.g., hours worked, people on payroll, wages, etc.) — must be equal to or better than that of its principal competitors.   Moreover, productivity must be continually increased, or a company risks a loss of competitiveness. These requirements motivate companies to invest in new technology, modern equipment and systems, and development support for employees for the purpose of increasing productivity.   Employees should be empowered to assure the quality of their work and to effect improvements in their work.

- *Reengineer business processes.*
  Generally speaking, the accepted approach for increasing productivity is to minimize the consumption of unproductive resources in the *strategic, core, support* and *administrative* work processes of the company.   This effort often entails the elimination of tasks and the *continuous learning* of new ways to work.   When tasks are removed from a process, these changes impact the remaining tasks in the process, thus changing the work performed by others.

- *Create an environment for learning[2].*
  As a result, process redesign often requires employees throughout companies to continually create and learn new

ways to do their work. In fact, the willingness and skill
with which employees respond to needed change in the
workplace have considerable bearing on the success of the
enterprise. The current emphasis on creating a *learning*[2] *organization* involves improving performance and increasing
productivity by having employees create and support the
continuous, planned change of the ways in which work is
accomplished.

6. **PREDOMINATE**
    The sixth and final objective of the Humaneering process is to
    achieve the strategic goal of establishing and sustaining an *or-
    ganizational competitive advantage* relative to competing entities,
    products and services — to *predominate* in the market. Achiev-
    ing competitive advantage based on other factors is short-lived
    in today's marketplace. Price, product feature, speed . . .
    eventually they make no difference. These advantages are eas-
    ily replicated by most competitors.

    - *Develop an organizational strategy.*
      In recent years, we have acquired considerable evidence
      that the organization may well be the remaining unique
      characteristic with which to distinguish a company from its
      competitors. The organization is the one aspect of *business
      competitiveness* that is enduring and not easily copied. With
      this perspective, some corporate leaders are making organ-
      izational performance and productivity a core strategy for
      their enterprise. And to do so, they are implementing a
      Humaneering process to assure that the entire company fo-
      cuses on maximizing human behavior, learning[2], perform-
      ance, productivity and advantage in appropriate ways.

    - *Identify and support leadership.*
      The challenge in this stage is finding the leadership within
      the organization that is required to make the application of
      Humaneering a reality. Not unlike TQM or other perva-
      sive initiatives, emphasis on organizational productivity
      begins at the top of the organization, where the authority is
      located. Though most of the work does occur within the
      normal operations of the organization, you can be sure that
      not much will happen if the application of Humaneering is

not a top priority of senior management. As Stephen Covey is fond of saying, "First things first."

This has been a very brief tour of the Humaneering process algorithm. Undoubtedly you recognize activity that now goes on in your organization . . . many companies do some of these right things now . . . but more often they are not coordinated and the goal is unclear. Few companies, however, would be starting from zero. From what clients tell me, the most helpful aspect of this process is that it first integrates all the activity that is intended to advance human behavior, learning[2], performance, productivity and competitiveness, and then separates it into distinguishable objectives that can be more easily accomplished. Without such a process to align all this activity, few people recognize the impact of their seemingly isolated handling of people-related issues. Isolated, unsupportive actions easily become costly barriers to success further along in the process . . . when it is no longer possible to correct the mistake or to see who is responsible.

Developing Organizational Competitive Advantage

The more common view of organizational issues suggests that just a single problem is responsible for missed goals, and that the solution is as simple as a single theory, approach or program. Organizational challenges are not so easily solved, yet we want to believe they are, if for no other reason than to simplify our lives. In fact, every activity in an organization is in some way interrelated to everything else in the organization. Every aspect of the organization is changing, causing changes, or being changed by everything that transpires within it. This complexity can be baffling.

The search for and the selection and preparation of employees have tremendous impact on the performance, productivity and competitive advantage achieved by an enterprise. Falling down on any one objective, even partially, will have adverse consequences that cannot be reversed even by extra effort later in this process. Therefore, each individual within the organization must share responsibility for the success of the Humaneering process—a concerted effort that can be accomplished only by establishing a corporate strategy to make the organization a competitive advantage. If the success of this strategy is made the objective of every employee, then it will be successful.

In regard to product or service quality, this concept is referred to as "controlling variance at the source."

Guess what happens when even well-intentioned members of the organization (1) do not understand what kind of people are best suited to the organization's work, (2) do not hire people with the right attitude and general capability, (3) fail to adequately prepare people for the work they will attempt to perform, (4) do not assign people to tasks designed for performance, (5) do not provide a motivating environment or engineer processes for productivity, and (6) do not focus the organization on establishing competitive advantage. All or any one of these omissions will negatively affect a company's performance, productivity and competitive advantage. Missed learning, poor performance, low productivity and *dis*advantage are results few firms can tolerate in today's competitive environment.

Now that you grasp the vital linkage of the elements in the Humaneering process, the next four chapters provide further discussion of the last four elements of this algorithm. These chapters might at first appear to be in the wrong order. Though they are in reverse order in contrast to the above explanation of the entire process, they will be presented in the order in which they must be approached for design and implementation: PREDOMINATE, PRODUCE, PERFORM, and PREPARE. This order follows the line of authority for setting strategy and making decisions in most companies—from top to bottom—because each element of the algorithm necessarily establishes a context and the objective for the elements preceding it in the algorithm.

8

Humaneering for Advantage

Humaneering (hyoo'me-nîr'ing) n. 1. The application of scientific principles concerning human beings, in particular their motivations, capacities and achievements, to practical ends, such as the design, formation and operation of effective and efficient processes, systems, and organizations. —vt.1. To plan, construct, manage, and accomplish practical results by way of skillful acts or ingenious plan to apply the scientifically validated capabilities of people.

James S. Pepitone
Humaneering: Human Performance Technology at Work (1989)

In years past, executives and managers did not concern themselves about *science* unless it related to their product or service. Even though they unknowingly depended on scientific knowledge concerning people and their behavior at work, these corporate chiefs have traditionally chosen to leave any explicit references to science to the experts. In view of their apparent success, they reasoned that they knew well enough from experience and common sense what they were doing when it came to people. As long as they were not challenged with a problem they had never seen before . . . if that was even possible . . . there was no reason to question their time-tested methods of management.

This familiar predisposition is at once understandable and inexplicable. It is understandable when we consider the experience and proven capability of most managers, and accept the accountability that they, not we, must assume for their roles and responsibilities. Just given the complexity of their job, we too would be tempted to focus on concerns for which we already have skills, from which we get the most enjoyment, and for which we are most likely rewarded. This seeming disinterest in human performance and organizational productivity is also understandable when we consider the undertreatment of organizational issues at all but a few of the top business schools. Even recent curriculum changes in the MBA programs at Harvard, Chicago, Wharton and others fail to recognize the potential of organizations to become a potent competitive advantage.* Furthermore, managers have been prodded and preached to concerning their organizational behavior since the "human relations school" theories made their way through major U.S. companies, yet their standards for success continued to focus on bottom-line results.

At the same time, this predisposition to treat the current wealth of organizational technology so lightly is inexplicable. Executives and managers are, as organization leaders, engaged in a very difficult, rather abstract, highly intellectual activity that ultimately depends on all the keen insight, accuracy and quickness of judgment they can muster. If these agents of the stakeholders neglect the continuously accumulating science concerning "people at work," are they not engaging in a form of Russian roulette—an act of reckless bravado—with their companies' human capital? Which is it—management malpractice, irresponsibility, negligence, incompetence, short-sightedness, carelessness, laziness, ignorance, convenience or simply a lack of motivation? Perhaps . . . but I do not think any of these possible explanations apply. Rather, I believe this prejudice of executives and managers against scientific knowledge is due to the complexity of this knowledge and to its presentation.

Emerging organizational technology must be sought after in the context of many different sciences—psychology, sociology, anthropology, education, economics and engineering, to name several—and in the text of conspicuously arcane scientific journals that seem almost irreconcilable with a manager's legitimate concerns for the bottom line. Not that there is anything particularly wrong with the methodology of the scientific pursuit of knowledge. Rather, the difficulty is in how this emerging knowledge is presented to the business community. The

---

* I know of only one graduate business school that officially recognizes this opportunity and effectively teaches students its cultivation. That is the Graduate School of Business and Management at Pepperdine University in Malibu, California, whose pioneering emphasis on the strategic management of organizational change and adult practitioner-focused instructional methods combine to create programs uniquely capable of teaching this knowledge and these skills to managers. Two other schools highly regarded for their emphasis on organizational management and change are the Weatherhead School of Management at Case Western Reserve University in Cleveland, Ohio, and the Graduate School of Management at Brigham Young University in Provo, Utah.

accessibility, format and jargon of academic journals, in particular, do not well serve executives and managers who must contend with a multitude of concerns and have little time for such reading. Nor does it well serve functional specialists who must integrate and present this knowledge, because they are already discounted as (and probably are) overly biased to developments in their area of specialization.

This is roughly how the problem was laid out to PBP in 1989 by the COO of a $2 billion consumer products firm. He was genuinely troubled by his organization's inability to effectively use emerging organizational technology to improve performance and increase productivity . . . particularly in the non-manufacturing areas of the company. Upon examination, we were able to confirm this condition and trace its root cause to the prohibitive difficulty experienced by executives and managers in accessing, understanding, relating, and applying this technology. Frequent attempts to introduce to the organization various elements of this advanced knowledge as it emerged always seemed to lack relevance and integration with current practices, even after an extensive program of costly and time-consuming training. Management had become hopeful only six months before when a training simulation had been effective in raising the consciousness of many managers to several management practices previously unquestioned, yet management was disappointed once again when little change had resulted. This last failure had prompted the COO's call for help.

PBP was offered the challenge (1) to equip the top 3,000 executives and managers of the company with a working knowledge of the "latest" in organizational technology, and (2) to facilitate the strategic redesign of the company's organizational subsystem (i.e., processes, structure and management systems) for the express purpose of attaining a sustainable organizational competitive advantage. This client engagement ultimately led to PBP's development of the science of Humaneering and the Humaneering process algorithm, as alluded to in Chapter 7. It further led to the development of a significant practice area for PBP, as other companies learned of the impact of this work. In summary, we found that executives and managers alike, once exposed to this integrated and straightforward presentation of relevant scientific knowledge about people at work, quickly "see" the potency of this knowledge and become energized to apply it to accomplish their objectives.

I am not so presumptive as to think that Humaneering will be declared a formal science anytime soon. However, it does provide a very helpful framework for integrating extensive technology on

Figure 8.1
The PREDOMINATE Stage
The Humaneering Process for Developing Organizational Competitive Advantage

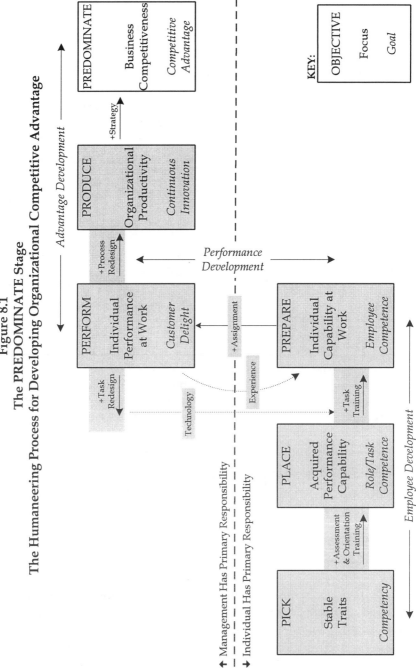

enhancing human accomplishment in the workplace. Furthermore, "humans seem to gain a sense of satisfaction in classifying things into compartments with solid barriers" (Strahler, 1992), and Humaneering seems to provide such comfort and confidence for executives and managers. For Human Resources and Training practitioners, the Humaneering process algorithm holds the promise of clarifying and enhancing their understanding of the cumulative process for achieving organizational competitive advantage, and the incorporated processes for supporting learning, improving performance and increasing productivity. With this understanding, they will add to their own learning, performance and productivity, and to that of their clients.

The PREDOMINATE Stage

Business competitiveness is the focus of the PREDOMINATE stage of the Humaneering process algorithm. (See **Figure 8.1.**) Nothing is more fundamental to any enterprise than its need to be competitive in its chosen markets. Because of this strategic importance, the responsibility for competitiveness is most often retained by the senior officers of a corporation. Only they have the range of options to assure that the enterprise takes every action required to sustain its business competitiveness, or to advance its competitive position at the expense of a careless competitor.

Achieving the PREDOMINATE stage objective of an organizational *competitive advantage* is contingent on this aim becoming a corporate strategy. Competitiveness is sufficiently critical to business that it is the responsibility of senior executives. Since the late 1970s, strategic management theorists have ascribed competitive advantage to external characteristics inherent in a firm's industry or markets. The underlying premise was that the market or industry imposed selective pressures, and firms that successfully adapted to those requirements would survive and grow, whereas those that did not adapt were doomed to failure. Managerial competencies and organizational effectiveness were implicitly reduced to elements of labor input. These theories have weakened considerably in recent years, because they failed to explain how the long-term effectiveness of individual companies contributed significantly to their achieving significant advantages in inherently weak industries and markets. New views of competitive strategy that emerged in the mid-1980s suggested that firm-specific organizational factors (1) contribute to profits independent of economic factors,

(2) contribute at twice the profit rates of economic factors, (3) are available to firms without limitation for their industry or market, and (4) have superior advantages as a sustainable competitive advantage.

The PREDOMINATE stage objective of designating organizational competitive advantage as a corporate strategy in turn establishes a context for the PRODUCE stage objective of increasing *organizational productivity*. Sustaining a persistent effort to increase productivity, particularly in light of the large number of failed reengineering attempts that have been documented in the business press, will require the emphasis given only to corporate strategy. (See **Figure 8.1**.)

The Concept of Corporate Strategy

Without question, the highest function of an executive is leading the continuous process of molding the attributes of an organization that generate, govern and achieve its purposes. Commingled with this lofty role is the formidable challenge to keep quarterly earnings increasing regularly to support stock prices and the stakeholders who provide their capital to the enterprise one day at a time. Granted, this challenge often calls for improvisatory action. However, it also calls for effective strategic management, or there will be no ace to play when a competitor slips, the market opens up to the company's way of thinking, or management needs to cover a sizable investment that went sour. Companies cannot back aggressive growth, turn around a bad quarter, and keep the customers "wowed," as Tom Peters says, without considerable effort on the front end. No such organizations exist without first having a corporate strategy to create this result.

Having that extra capability in reserve is reassuring, is it not? I guess that makes leading a company a little like driving a car. You probably do not make a habit of driving your Porsche at 100 miles per hour. But when the semi is barreling down the on-ramp and headed your way, it is nice to know you can punch the accelerator and forget the truck. That is the good news. What about the organization that wants the CEO to "go fly a kite" or engage in some other questionable recreation? What kind of "kick" is that organization going to have when the going gets tough? Just like the reserve power of a car, the responsiveness of an organization cannot be taken lightly . . . not without significant risk.

Corporate strategy is the result of the complex functions and responsibilities of the senior management in a company; the crucial problems that affect the success of the total enterprise; and the decisions that determine its direction, shape its future, and produce the results desired. According to Harvard professor Kenneth R. Andrews, these executives are faced with an unending array of concerns, including

> *the choice of purposes, the development and recognition of organization identity and character, the unending definition of what needs to be done, the mobilization of resources for the attainment of goals in the face of aggressive competition or adverse circumstances, and the definitions of standards for the enforcement of responsible and ethical behavior* (1987).

As senior executives know only too well, the determination of suitable *objectives* provides focus and makes possible a rational choice among alternatives. They are peppered with proposals, suggestions and inferences promoting every conceivable goal and activity. For executives to do their work, they must formulate an appropriate pattern of purpose and policy, and must determine how plans will be converted into results. That is the role of strategy.

There are functional strategies to guide functions, business strategies to guide product and market choices, and corporate strategies that are comprehensive enough to incorporate both. Corporate strategy also encompasses longer-term and more-pervasive goals of the company, issues that require the single-minded convergence of individual effort throughout the organization. Well-designed corporate strategy distinguishes every company from its competitors and establishes a competitive advantage. By arriving at such clarity of purpose, executives are then able to focus their full attention, energy and influence on its fulfillment. Powerful ideas that do not find their way into corporate strategy never seem to get the support required by the organization to have them take shape.

A central role for corporate strategy is to keep business managers focused on the same chosen paths for achieving the goals of the enterprise. Clearly articulated corporate strategy provides guiding clarification of the character and purposes of the company to all its operations. Likewise, corporate strategy is intended to focus the technical knowledge of staff-support specialists in the same direction as management, rather than in the direction of their undoubtedly more interesting concerns with technical functions. How else can management direct the effective use of science without actually needing to know it? Quite probably, there is no better way.

A Strategy for Organizational Advantage

Take, for example, the suggestion that enlightened and opportunistic companies should have an explicit corporate strategy *to transform the organization into a competitive advantage.* Perhaps it is necessary to be even more specific—to say that the advantage will be low cost, product quality, extraordinary service, or some other superlative—so there is no question how managers should mold the future organization. The danger in too narrow a specification, however, is that it produces a lopsided organization that is superior in the target feature but otherwise weak. No, it seems important for the focus to be on well-rounded performance. The best way to achieve this goal would be to have several measures that capture the balance desired . . . just as it is wise to balance sales-volume objectives with profit-margin objectives.

To determine whether having a corporate strategy *to transform the organization into a competitive advantage* is a smart decision, consider the impact of *not* having such a corporate strategy. Not having a corporate strategy for the organization is more likely the case for most companies, anyway.

First, we can reasonably surmise that *not* having such a strategy would lead even the most business-wise and well-intentioned managers to give no more interest and attention to the organization as a point of focus and accountability than they would to office space, furniture or any other reasonably abundant resource necessary to operate just about any business. Strategy creates focus, and the absence of strategy assures the absence of focus. Particularly when personal security is involved, expectations drive perception and behavior. Just as no manager wants to be the one who forgets about the company's strategy, or who performs poorly in working toward a strategic objective, it makes little sense for managers to emphasize issues that are not considered important by the people making the *big* decisions. Mature corporate executives are aware of the focusing potential of measured and financially rewarded goals; this is not a new concept.

Second, we can surmise that it is impractical to make every goal a corporate strategy—the idea is to focus everyone on a few key success factors that, if accomplished, will achieve the company's purposes. Is the goal of organizational competitive advantage sufficiently potent that reaching it should be one of the few key strategies of any business? Though no one is capable of answering that question for the management actually accountable, we can examine some recent research to help in making this judgment. Current strategic management literature offers insight into the factors that contribute to establishing a sustainable competitive advantage. Three studies highlight several of these findings:

- *Organizational factors are independent of economic factors in determining firm performance, and contribute twice as much in firm profit rates.*

  Gary Hansen and Birger Wernerfelt, professors at the University of Washington and the Sloan School at MIT, respectively, examined the firm profitability of 60 Fortune 1000 firms and were able to separate the profit contribution based on *organizational* factors (i.e., structure, motivation, decision-making, leadership and other factors making up organizational climate) from the profit contribution based on *economic* factors (i.e., industry return-on-assets (ROA), market share, and organization size). They determined that these two factors were *independent*, and that the organizational factors contributed about *twice the variance* in firm profit rates. They conclude,

  > Our findings have important managerial implications. Top management teams that can demonstrate excellence in both areas – competitive positioning in the market place and building organizational context – will do significantly better than those that strive for more unidimensional concepts of excellence. Additionally, it would suggest that the critical issue in firm success and development is not primarily the selection of growth industries or product niches, but is the building of an effective, directed, human organization (1989).

- *Human and organizational capital resources are uniquely suitable as a source of sustainable competitive advantage.*

  Jay Barney, a professor at Texas A&M University, examined the suitability of various firm resources to establish sustained competitive advantage. Previous research in this area by Michael Porter of Harvard, and others, attributes advantage to the characteristics of industries, making the implicit assumption that firms within an industry or strategic grouping are identical in terms of the resources they control and the strategies they pursue. This assumption fails to factor in any consideration of a firm's *distinctive attributes* and the ways in which they contribute to competitive position. Barney's research questions this omission, and further establishes the following criteria for determining *sources of sustainable competitive advantage*:

1. *Valuable* for improving efficiency and effectiveness
2. *Rare* among competitors
3. *Inimitable* due to one or more of the following:
   - Unique history of the firm
   - Advantage not understood by competitors
   - Advantage based on social complexity
4. *Unique* beyond strategically equivalent substitutes

When the three principal categories of firm resources listed below are evaluated with these criteria, the unique suitability of *human* and *organizational* capital resources becomes readily apparent:

1. *Physical capital* - physical technology, plant and equipment, geographic location, and access to raw materials
2. *Human capital* - training, experience, judgment, intelligence, relationships, and insight of individual managers and workers in a firm
3. *Organizational capital* - formal reporting structure, formal and informal planning, and controlling and coordinating systems, as well as informal relations among groups within a firm and between a firm and those in its environment

As Barney concludes,

> *What becomes clear is that firms cannot expect to "purchase" sustained competitive advantages on open markets. Rather, such advantages must be found in the rare, imperfectly imitable, and non-substitutable resources already controlled by a firm. Managers are important . . .*

*for it is managers that are able to understand and describe
the economic performance potential of a firm's endow-
ments. Without such managerial analyses, sustained
competitive advantage is not likely* (1991).

- *Firms have the capacity through managerial proactiveness to
  create organizational competencies that generate a sustainable
  competitive advantage.*

Research conducted by Augustine Lado (Cleveland State University), Nancy Boyd (University of North Texas) and Peter
Wright (Memphis State University) demonstrates the limitations to strategic thinking that ascribes competitive advantage
solely to market and industry characteristics, and their findings
substantiate the conclusion that a firm's *distinctive organizational
competencies* are, in fact, *superior* sources of sustainable competitive advantage. Drawing on research in interpretive sociology, cognitive psychology and behavioral economics, Lado, et
al., establish that firms have the capacity to create and grasp
opportunities, and in particular recognize managerial proactiveness in influencing business performance. They identify
four sources of firm-specific *distinctive organizational competencies* not subject to imitation:

1. *Managerial competencies and strategic focus* - the articulated strategic vision becomes the fulcrum around
   which the firm's unique competencies may be developed . . . and effective implementation depends on the
   extent to which a firm's managers acquire and mobilize
   specialized strategic resources that may yield superior
   returns relative to those of competitors.
2. *Resource-based competencies* - these consist of core
   human and nonhuman assets, such as rent-generating
   skills and capabilities, that allow a firm to outperform
   rival firms over a sustained period of time . . . and are
   causally ambiguous, impeding competitor imitation.
3. *Transformation-based strategies* - these may encom-
   pass *innovation* — the capability to generate new products and processes faster than competitors can; and
   organizational culture — the capacity for organizational
   learning, change and adaptation.

4. *Output-based competencies* - these include the firm's physical outputs that deliver value to customers, and more importantly, the "invisible" outputs, such as reputation for quality, brand name, and dealer networks, all of which provide value to customers.

Their findings indicate that *managerial competencies* and *strategic focus* are largely responsible for attracting specialized resources that are synergistically combined, transformed, and channeled to clients in ways which generate a sustainable competitive advantage to the firm. This strategy requires managerial investment in causally ambiguous organizational competencies that are characterized by

- *tacitness* - competencies that are not easily explained or replicated.
- *complexity* - competencies that involve interrelated skills and knowledge.
- *specificity* - competencies in skills that are not easily transferable to alternate use.

Lado, et al., conclude that

> *a strong organizational culture unleashes human creative potential to generate a continuous stream of ideas that may be translated into new products and processes. At the same time it permits realization of scale economies and incremental learning by encouraging and rewarding "volition, imaginativeness and drive" in the implementation of efficiency- and innovation-enhancing strategies. Top management contributes to the ongoing delivery of value by specifying standards of performance, communicating these clearly and unambiguously to employees, establishing appropriate hiring, training, motivation, and reward systems for developing core skills, and boosting employee morale — developing and nurturing their firms' idiosyncratic competencies that inhibit imitability (1992).*

This research, as well as other studies too numerous to mention, points to a consequential shift in our knowledge about the sources of sustainable competitive advantage. It has become clear that management is not restricted to accepting the competitive standing that is implicit in the merits of the industry or market of the enterprise, as was believed in the earliest days of strategic management thinking. In fact, potential sustainable competitive advantage is most readily found in the unique characteristics of effective organizations.

When and How, Not If

This finding presents you, the reader, with knowledge that few managers have come to learn and appreciate. The early timing of this counsel further extends its benefit—adding "first mover advantages"—to the first firm in an industry or market to implement a corporate strategy *to transform the organization into a competitive advantage*. These firms may gain access to new customers, develop a positive reputation, improve strategic services, increase productivity, or raise performance standards across the board—all before other firms implement similar strategies. As it becomes clearer to a growing number of senior management teams that *organizational competitive advantage* may ultimately be the only truly sustainable competitive advantage, some of the opportunity will be gone.

Perhaps the prevailing issue is not whether a firm should have a corporate strategy for organizational advantage. The more relevant question is selecting the organizational areas in which to first improve performance and productivity. Sales, front-line services, middle management, or staff services—all are likely prospects for a significant ramp-up in competitive performance in any company. Based on my 17 years of consulting experience, I have learned that there is not a human function in any company that cannot be improved dramatically. The only ingredient that is necessary is for management to make it a strategic priority—a corporate strategy.

"How?" is the next logical question, and the answer is "to follow the Humaneering process algorithm and provide the needed process support at each stage." Followed one step at a time, the algorithm will guide the transformation of the human and organizational competencies in any company function.

The first step of the Humaneering process is the decision discussed in this chapter: management's decision to transform the organization into a competitive advantage.

9

Innovating for Productivity

Our grandfathers worked six days a week
to earn what most of us now earn by Tuesday afternoon.
The ferment in management will continue
until we build organizations that are more consistent
with man's higher aspirations beyond food, shelter and belonging.

Bill O'Brien
CEO, Hanover Insurance

Productivity is a fundamental concept central to the survival and development of enterprise and to the prosperity of employees. Adam Smith outlined in *The Wealth of Nations* the direct relationship between value produced and wages, and explained that it was through continuously improving their capability that workers could produce increasingly greater value and thus increase their wages. He further explained that workers who did not increase their productive ability in their chosen occupation, or shift their occupation to one which was valued more highly, would see their wages decrease as time passed. As consequential as productivity is, it remains a concept that is not well understood, even among employees.

Productivity relates the cost *input* of all major resources involved in production to the value *output* they produce. For any organization, there are many such resources—including people, facilities, equipment, money, materials and vendor services—going into the operations of a business. There are also several outputs, including products, services, information and *waste*. Ideally, the contribution of each resource to production should increase steadily; however, the essential goal is increased productivity overall. The most direct approach known to increase productivity is the innovation of process-level work methods that reduce resource consumption.

An added investment in any one resource should result in a greater reduction of another resource or a greater contribution in output, or both. Furthermore, the cumulative result should offset the increased expense *and* reward the additional investment. There would be no reason to make investments in existing processes if this were not the case. For example, an investment in the form of a wage increase must result in either of two outcomes: (1) a greater reduction of another resource, such as reduced staffing or vendor services, or (2) a greater output, such as increased production or services rendered. And the cumulative benefit of these outcomes needs to be greater than the investment . . . to provide an incentive to invest—an ROI.

Thus for employees to justify an increase in wages, it is necessary that they generate a greater reduction in the expense for some other resource or generate greater work output, or do both, to create an impact that (1) offsets the increased cost and (2) rewards the investment. And because investors and management must strive to minimize the risk associated with investments, this same principle is prudently applied in reverse: *only* when managers receive evidence of increased output do they know that they can reward employees with increased wages without reducing profitability.

Moreover, it makes no sense to change one factor at the expense of another. For example, an investment in additional equipment should not result in an *increase* in labor costs . . . although this is exactly what happened as a result of investments in micro-computers in the 1980s—white-collar productivity decreased because people had to spend so much time figuring out how to productively use this new labor-saving device.

Systematic, continuous increases in productivity are essential to the competitive enterprise. Without such increases, firms quickly lose their competitiveness and risk eventual demise. Firms with extraordinary increases in productivity can increase profits, attract new sources of financial capital, invest in new plant and equipment, increase worker wages *and* attain a significant competitive advantage in the marketplace.

The PRODUCE Stage

Organizational productivity is the focus of the PRODUCE stage of the Humaneering process algorithm. (See **Figure 9.1.**) The need to continually increase productivity throughout the organization makes productivity an important objective of all employees, regardless of their specific work role. This need requires that everyone in the organization be committed to process-level innovation—the principal method of increasing productivity—which, in turn, necessitates the rethinking of how task-level work is accomplished and the creation of new ways to work with greater effectiveness and efficiency.

Achieving the PRODUCE stage goal of continuous innovation is contingent on the leadership that is established in the PREDOMINATE stage. Though productivity improvement is highly contingent on people—requiring human ingenuity, affecting the design of human work and depending on the support of employees—it is an abstract concept not often measured at the individual performer level, and thus often difficult for people to comprehend and effect. Productivity is one of the six objectives in the Humaneering process algorithm because it is only one of many important concerns competing for the attention of employees. Executives and managers have to establish productivity improvement as a prominent organizational objective for it to receive proper attention from their employees, who are characteristically ingenious and efficient, and are therefore likely to do as little as possible to get a job done (Simon, 1976). A corporate strategy to achieve organizational competitive advantage provides the needed context. Without such a *manifesto* to capture the concern of employees, one can assume that this priority will receive little direct attention.

The PRODUCE stage focus on increasing organizational productivity in turn establishes a context for the PERFORM stage focus on having all employees achieve high levels of *individual performance at work*. Focusing the organization on a constant challenge to *increase productivity* establishes a ubiquitous concern for innovation at the *process level* of work, which often generates a corresponding need to redesign *task-level* work that *improves performance*. Efforts to increase productivity will frequently result in performance improvements at the same time; however, it is unacceptable for performance improvements to reduce productivity, or for productivity increases to reduce performance levels. Without the integration of these two objectives, as provided by the Humaneering process algorithm, people often do not grasp the distinctions between these important interventions, and each

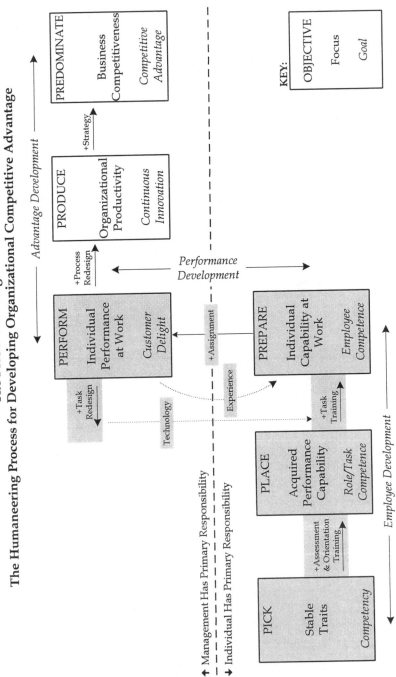

Figure 9.1
The PRODUCE Stage
The Humaneering Process for Developing Organizational Competitive Advantage

is then easily accomplished to the detriment of the other. **Figure 9.2** clarifies the relationship between task-level interventions to improve performance and process-level interventions to increase productivity.

Innovating Processes for Increased Productivity

As you undoubtedly know if you have ever worked in a bureaucratic organization, a vast amount of resources is consumed *un*productively by what goes on between functions and between people to coordinate the work processes in organizations. Bureaucracies are designed purposely with work processes made up of labyrinthine systems and procedures in order to provide for the standardization, specialization and control of the organization itself. As a result, the challenge to redesign organizational processes to minimize the consumption of unproductive resources calls for virtually everyone in organizations to find better, more efficient ways to work together.

    Organizations meet this challenge by accomplishing the following:

1. *Reengineering business processes*
   Employees are organized into cross-functional teams to focus on the redesign of important business processes. A *process* is defined as a series of tasks or steps that receive *inputs* (materials, information, people, machines, methods) and produce *outputs* (physical products, information, services) designed for specific purposes. These cross-functional teams then design from scratch new high-performance processes that (1) produce product and service outputs that delight customers, (2) optimize the utilization of resources provided by the marketplace, and (3) restructure the relevant parts of the organization to optimize the process output.

2. *Creating an environment for innovation (learning[2])*
   Management must generate a supportive climate that values innovation, learning[2] and change. This objective is accomplished only by genuine efforts to involve employees, encourage their empowerment, create a shared vision, provide clear performance expectations and non-punitive feedback, provide learning[2] resources, and reward performance and contribution.

Figure 9.2
Comparison of Improvement Interventions

Label	Focus	Goal*	Strategy	Severity
Reengineering	Process level work *Organizational Subsystem*	Increase organizational productivity *Continuous Innovation*	Restructure process to minimize unproductive resource consumption through the elimination of task-level work.	Radical change 40-90%
Redesign	Task level work *Work Subsystem*	Improve work performance *Customer Delight*	Redesign task to achieve customer standards of performance and minimize variance from them.	Significant change 10-40%
Continuous Improvement	Work outputs *Role/Job or Task/Skill Elements*	Enhance product/service quality *Customer Delight*	Refine work outputs to continuously improve products/services.	Incremental change 1-10%

* Reengineering, redesign and continuous improvement are capable of providing increased quality, lower costs, increased speeds, reduced capital requirements, etc.

Though processes will differ somewhat from industry to industry, and even from company to company within an industry, there are four *core* processes upon which the success of companies depends:

1. Product-development process
2. Order-generation process
3. Order-fulfillment process
4. Customer-service process

All other processes, such as human resources processes, management processes, information systems processes, and legal processes, exist to support and measure the success of these four core processes.

Achieving a Radical Redesign of Work

Since World War II, the emphasis on increasing productivity has been directed toward factory labor, although it has been a steadily declining part of the entire U.S. workforce since the peak of wartime production. After the war, we witnessed the rapid expansion of white-collar employment as organizations continued to expand. Coupled with the decrease in factory labor, this great increase in white-collar jobs has precipitated a dramatic shift in the makeup of the workforce in the past 50 years. Furthermore, a rapid expansion in technology has added sophistication to almost every area of white-collar work, such that these white-collar workers are now the *knowledge and service specialists* that dominate the workforce.

Improving the productivity of knowledge and service workers will be a greater challenge yet. Unlike the success achieved in increasing the productivity of factory and transportation labor–a respectable four percent increase compounded over the past 125 years–the greatest gains are likely to come from changes in the work environment rather than changes in the tasks themselves (Drucker, 1993). These gains can be attributed to the very different nature of this work, which, when compared with work in previous generations, is based more on acquired intelligence, cognitive ability, relationship skills and discretionary effort. Taylor's strategies for improving the efficiency of machinelike factory labor in the 1920s have already proven themselves *in*effective with today's more sophisticated workforce.

The reengineering initiative is just the beginning of monumental changes that will take place in the workplace during the balance of this decade, and probably thereafter. It focuses work design on the overall process that best achieves the end goal, rather than on the design and control of individuals or tasks. Reengineering focuses principally on restructuring the organization from a functional form to some other form that orients workers toward achieving the best performance and productivity from a business process. Typically, such restructuring involves a redistribution of tasks, information and people to facilitate a new, more efficient process.

When this radical redesign of work is accomplished in a positive environment by people insulated from the threat of job loss, and notwithstanding task and job changes for just about everybody, then the majority of employees agree that (1) such restructuring makes sense and (2) it is well overdue for most of the work that goes on in today's organizations. These prerequisites are important, however, and their omission easily explains much of the trouble that firms have encountered with their reengineering efforts. Only savvy leaders have avoided reengineering failures by recognizing the importance of organization members for their exclusive capacity to provide these key forms of support to reengineering initiatives:

1. *Design support* - to combine their individual perspectives and talents in a collaborative team effort
2. *Support for change* - to generate their support for the changes that are required
3. *Implementation support* - to simplify, speed up and assure effective implementation

Though natural learners in terms of their inborn capabilities, people are reluctant to innovate more productive ways of doing their work or to initiate other changes for the sake of their firms when such actions only increase their feelings of insecurity. Moreover, many people become accustomed to their current way of working and prefer for it to continue without change. This understanding suggests, then, that the resistance management is witnessing is at once natural and a response to the overall climate of the organization.

In many organizations, management has failed to accurately assess employee attitudes toward organizations and managers, drawing the unwarranted conclusion that employees are far more positive than they are in fact. Management's attempts to get organization members to support reengineering and to work as teams on this challenge have in many cases consisted of only authority-based direction and resource support . . . hardly motivation for insecure employees to initiate changes that will either increase their work or put them out of work. In the climate of many firms, leadership is more likely to draw the response of people "going through the motions" — with no substantial work being done, or even less. Adding to this predicament, the mid-level managers to whom most employees look for direction and motivation are more at risk than other segments of the workforce. These managers have been given little to gain and much to lose, even further reducing the chances for successful reengineering.

The reengineering of work has just begun, and so far only the critical performance areas are receiving attention. The great challenge that firms are experiencing with this initiative will slow down the competitive pressures that will ultimately result from successful reengineering efforts. At some point in the future, every aspect of organizational work can benefit from such redesign. However, this transformation can happen only if management figures out that this work is dependent on people, and can be accomplished only in a generative environment that promotes learning, continuous change and professional development.

Energizing Organizations

The performance, productivity and competitive advantage of organizations — whether we are speaking of the organization as a whole, as groups, or as individual employees — have become much more essential to the success of any enterprise. For executives and managers, organizations are no longer simply a concern of human relations. Each individual employee in an organization either adds to or subtracts from the outcome, and therefore creates the margin of success or failure in accomplishing the objective of the enterprise. Nonetheless, Drucker reminds some of us that the primary purpose of organizations is not simply to exist, to provide jobs, or to achieve any social purpose; organizations exist to produce results:

> *An organization is a HUMAN GROUP, composed of specialists working together on a common task. Unlike society, community, or family — the traditional social aggregates — organization is purposefully designed and grounded neither in the psychological nature of human beings nor in biological necessity (1993).*

Not inconsistent with this definition, organizations also help people to meet their human needs and to achieve their human goals . . . which is precisely why people are willing to focus themselves on the accomplishment of their organizations' tasks (Knowles, 1980). With the evolution of our post-industrial society, however, the increased prosperity and sophistication of the U.S. workforce have gradually shifted the nature of people's orientation toward work—changing what they need and want for their services. Daniel Yankelovich makes this same assertion in his provocative text, *New Rules: Searching for Self-fulfillment in a World Turned Upside Down.* He explains that people have advanced from their prior "instrumental" view of work, in which work is simply a way to earn a paycheck, to a more "sacred" view, in which people seek more "intrinsic" benefits (1981). If we compare the knowledge workers of today with the factory workers of 1900, or with the "organization men" in post-World War II bureaucratic organizations, we can appreciate that their human needs from work have evolved to a point well beyond a paycheck—they have effectively climbed Maslow's hierarchy to such needs as respect, accomplishment and self-development.

Correspondingly, when people feel that their needs are not being met, that they are not receiving support for the achievement of their goals, or that they are being mistreated, they withdraw—either psychologically or physically, either passively or aggressively—and withhold their services from their organizations. Consider it a law of *reciprocity*—a straightforward *quid pro quo*. And this reaction is no less true for managers than for any other employee group. Reciprocity is standard market-system behavior—behavior that managers can well understand . . . behavior they see in suppliers and customers . . . behavior they can predict, plan for and accommodate. Reciprocity does not give managers control in an authoritarian sense, which may be a common desire in the subconscious of many managers, but it certainly is control in a rational sense. Reciprocity is simply a mutual or cooperative interchange of favors, rights and privileges; or two or more people exchanging what they have for what they want or need. This is precisely how the market economy was described by Adam Smith, and how it still works today.

The difficulty managers faced in the 1950s—when it became clear that money and benefits alone could not buy the full effort of employees—was in not understanding *what* employees wanted. This lack of understanding was innocent enough, as employees were equally unable to express their own evolving needs, wants and desires in market-rational terms.   At that time, the only real insight into employee-dissatisfaction problems was provided by developing psychosocial theories — hardly the type of facts managers were accustomed to using as their basis for decisions. With only recommendations for innocuous human-relations training in hand, and Elton Mayo's hypothesis that a little more attention paid to employees would solve the problem, management disingenuously agreed to the "training" solution, consequently launching the still-common practice of prescribing training for just about every kind of people problem experienced in organizations.

The Drive for Self-Betterment

The answer management was searching for can still be found in the wisdom of Adam Smith in a basic premise for the market system that he presented in *The Wealth of Nations*. The question is as relevant today as it was in 1776. Given the proposed economic freedom of workers, what would provide the *motive force* for individuals to learn new skills and develop their capabilities so they could meet the needs of their employers? Smith determined that workers would be motivated to develop the needed capabilities because of an innate human characteristic — *the drive for self-betterment*. Smith further asserted that advances in production technology would support workers by continuously improving their productivity, and that these gains would then yield increased wages and an ever-higher standard of living for workers.

Self-betterment, which must be defined by each individual, has demonstrated itself to be a predominant motivating force. This is even more the case among the somewhat more logical knowledge workers in today's workforce. Decisions regarding education, careers, employment, roles, and assignments correlate very highly with their perceptions of potential for both immediate and strategic self-improvement. *Effective support* for employees to develop their competencies to do the work required to accomplish the goals of the organization will lead to the realization of the goals of both the company and employees . . . to the extent that these competencies enable employees to better themselves. The net effect is *joint optimization*. For the organization, the goal is effective performance in creating customer value and continuous increases in productivity. For the employee, the goal is progress up the ladder of Maslow's "hierarchy of needs" — from survival, to safety, to affection, to esteem, to self-actualization, the ultimate goal.

The Learning² Organization

What constitutes effective support for employees to develop their competencies? When I ask this question of people with the responsibility to provide such support, why do I get a different answer than when I ask randomly selected employees the very same question? From executives, managers, and even Human Resources and Training practitioners, I get responses restricted to such topics as tuition reimbursement programs, performance management programs, course catalogs, and other traditional initiatives intended to support employees. From employees, however, the responses are as varied and unique as the people themselves. "Let me talk to the manufacturer of this machine"; "somebody help me figure out a way to work with those people"; "help me get into a master's (degree) program"; "my supervisor's brilliant . . . I'd just like to get some of his time"; and "evening and weekend courses so I don't have to take time off" are a few responses that I have received.

Notice the difference here? Employees invariably define their support needs in terms of improving their performance in their immediate work, and yet each has somewhat different needs. The people in charge of providing this support see these needs differently, and in terms of solutions that were conceived years ago for a very different workforce. Typically the support that is provided consists of highly structured initiatives, entry-level knowledge and skill support, and one-size-fits-all training programs. This approach may be easy to administer, but it cannot come close to meeting the development needs of an organization of knowledge and service specialists. Training was designed as an intervention to provide standardization — not to support development. People develop through experience, through doing their work to meet ever-increasing standards of performance. Furthermore, people have unique performance-support needs and different learning styles; they cannot be well served with the same solutions. What's more important . . . supporting employees, or having a program that can be easily administered?

Effective performance support for employees has to be defined in terms that maximize the development of every individual in the organization. Anything less will result in sub-optimal performance and will at some point not be competitive. Therefore, in order to satisfy everyone's development potential, management must provide an overall work environment that consistently supports the highest potential performance and productivity — an organizational system that is dedicated to helping people improve their performance and develop their capabilities — with learning[2] occurring as a natural by-product of work itself. Since effective support can be accomplished only by providing a work environment that facilitates learning[2], then the quality of learning[2] that takes place is affected by the kind of organization it is. The organization should not be seen simply as a place where training activities are provided; rather it should be envisioned as an environment that increases productivity because it supports learning[2] and performance improvement (Knowles, 1990). This is the "learning[2] organization" that astute leaders now strive to create.

Productivity Is Discretionary But Not Optional

There is no escaping the fact that it is both a competitive necessity and a responsibility of all organization members to strive continually for increases in productivity. Such increases must occur if firms are to survive and to increase their employees' wages. Major efforts recently launched to reengineer the core and support processes of organizations are long overdue, and they are only the beginning of massive changes forthcoming in the workplace. For organization members to meet this formidable challenge, however, executives and managers will need to acquire a new appreciation for their organizations and learn how to develop a more conducive environment for work. For organization members to provide their discretionary support, management must provide them with a work environment that is at once secure for the hard-working individual, innovative in its ever-changing approach to work and supportive of individual employee performance development.

The real lesson that needs to be learned about the individual employee's contribution to organizational productivity is that it is discretionary. Management that looks with antipathy at an oversized and uninspired organization has only itself to blame. If management could ask why employees are more often motivated to withhold their effort than to give it enthusiastically, they would hear — as I often do — the explanation of perfectly rational behavior that is adapting to processes, structures, and systems that retard rather than inspire a productive response. The process to increase productivity is not downsizing, and reengineering is only a start. Rather, it is the process of creating a "turned-on" organization, the fifth *core process* in the post-industrial company.

10

Working for Performance

As the role of performance improvement in organizations increasingly takes on strategic proportions through human resource development, quality improvement, reengineering, and performance technology, executives are being held more accountable in this arena. Their organizations spend millions of dollars each year on development efforts aimed at employees and customers. But while much is to be gained in terms of increased performance, money spent hastily on programs based on erroneous assumptions yields very little for the organizations and the individuals participating in them.

Richard A. Swanson
*Analysis for Improving
Performance* (1994)

Performance is the act of accomplishing some activity or thing. Performance is a relative term, measured as a percentage of an expectation—the extent to which expectations are met. Doing exactly what is expected is a 100-percent performance; doing half of what is expected is a 50-percent performance; and doing more than is expected would result in a performance in excess of 100 percent.

People commonly refer to performance in general terms that express a judgment, such as *good, bad, better, extraordinary, horrible, world class,* etc. Though some are more judgmental than others, people commonly judge the performance of just about everything—

He was late for work.
The show was awesome.
The weather is horrible.
I beat last year's quota by a mile.

She isn't the least bit cooperative.
The class was extraordinarily responsive.
Idiots . . . why can't they watch where they're going?

Such expressions—non-specific and judging—leave it to the listener (1) to interpret these general expressions of performance, and (2) to guess what the person's expectation was to begin with. As you can imagine, general judgments like these would not give employees a clear picture of work performance. For this reason, performance measures concerning work are often expressed in quantitative terms such as *85 percent completion, 106 percent of quota, 92 percent of standard,* etc.

These figures are calculated by dividing the result by the expectation:

RESULT ÷ EXPECTATION = PERFORMANCE

For some work, however, it is not reasonable or possible to state expectations and measure results in *quantitative* terms. For instance, how do you best measure the performance of a Trainer? The number of classes taught? The number of students? The test scores of the participants? The approval ratings of the students? None of these measures the real goal of Training.

In a situation like this, and probably in regard to the work of most knowledge and service specialists, we are forced to substitute *qualitative* terms—scales that describe a range of performance levels in words—to communicate expectations and to feed back results. Because these scales are not nearly as specific, and therefore not as clear, as quantitative terms, they are subject to broad variations in meaning. Furthermore, there is an ongoing debate as to whether performance expectations should focus on *observable behavior* or on *results*. But since people are unique individuals and there are many ways to accomplish any task, does it make sense to evaluate observable behavior? And since all work involves the input of many people, how logical or possible is it to measure individual performance in terms of results?

Though performance is frequently and casually mentioned in the workplace, the difficulties alluded to above indicate that performance is a *very complex* concept. In addition to concerns about measuring performance and communicating results in performance terms, other factors add considerably to the challenge to achieve high levels of performance in the workplace:

1. Whose expectations?
2. What to measure?
3. What creates current results?
4. What will improve performance?

The way these questions are answered has a major influence on the success of any enterprise. All too often, the answers are generated without full understanding of the subject. As a result, *expectations* are based on the judgment of an employee or manager, activity is the only *measure* of performance, *results* are attributed to the employees who last touch the product or perform the service, and training is the specified intervention to *improve performance*.

The PERFORM Stage

Individual performance at work is the focus of the PERFORM stage of the Humaneering process algorithm. (See **Figure 10.1.**) For an organization to be truly successful, all individuals need to perform their work to fulfill their part of one or more business processes. The shift from *productivity* to *performance* as the goal is a shift from organizational processes to individual tasks. Although individuals may have difficulty recognizing their influence on productivity because it is an organizational measure, performance is an important objective of all employees, regardless of their specific roles or tasks.

Achieving the PERFORM stage goal of *customer delight* is contingent on the *leadership* and *organizational priority* established in the PREDOMINATE stage and the *process focus* and *organizational environment* established in the PRODUCE stage. In turn, the PERFORM stage, in which all employees work at their highest *individual performance* level to *delight customers*, establishes a context for the focus on *individual capability at work* in the PREPARE stage.

Achieving high levels of performance throughout organizations requires that all organization members make the following commitments:

1. *Accept responsibility for results* - be accountable for (a) the overall performance of the enterprise, (b) the output of the processes to which they contribute and (c) their individual roles or tasks in these processes.

**Figure 10.1
The PERFORM Stage
The Humaneering Process for Developing Organizational Competitive Advantage**

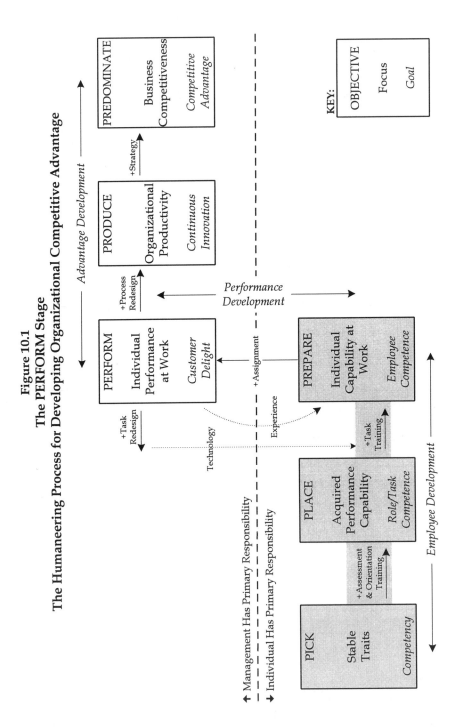

2. *Maintain high performance* - make every reasonable effort to perform in their roles or tasks (a) to the limit of their ability and (b) in a manner consistent with their required contribution to these processes.
3. *Support continuous improvement* - identify and support the implementation of improvements in (a) their role or tasks, (b) the processes to which they contribute and (c) the overall operations of the enterprise.

The PERFORM stage objective of achieving high levels of *individual performance at work* is highly contingent on people, as are the other stages of the Humaneering process algorithm. People either perform the work directly, or they operate, build, design, invent, order, install, and maintain equipment that does. In some way, people have a pivotal role in all work and in all performance levels reached.

For individuals to perform at competitive levels, there must be a continuous emphasis on improving individual performance. Each individual must focus equally on the continuous improvement of (1) role or task design, (2) resource availability and utilization and (3) human capability. Improvements need to stress the integration of "social" and "technical" factors to be successful. Though most organizations continuously stress work performance, managers have historically attributed *good* performance to machine capability and *poor* performance to human *in*capability. On several occasions, I have heard managers say unwittingly, "We'd have a great organization if it weren't for all these people." Perhaps we can empathize with managers by imagining ourselves in their role. When organizations are not designed for high performance, there is no doubt they can be very frustrating to manage.

Organizations as Whole and Open Systems

TQM initiatives have focused many organizations on improving individual performance at work. The work of Deming and Juran, and others, has made a great contribution to the performance of Japanese and U.S. companies.

Of all that management has learned from TQM, I think their greatest insight has come as the result of Deming's famous "red bead" exercise, in which he simulates the fact that performance improvement is achieved largely through *work design* and *changing the system*, rather than through steps to coerce or motivate workers. For this exercise, he typically selects volunteers from his audience and assigns them the task of withdrawing only white beads from a tray containing white and red beads, with a special tool designed for that purpose. They try, but cannot perform the task. Regardless of what they try, they cannot prevent red beads from getting in the tool. Deming then pokes fun at management's typical efforts to improve performance by taking the participants aside and in order encouraging, scolding, training and offering an incentive to them in an effort to improve their performance. Of course, none of these initiatives can improve their performance because the real problem is work design. The individuals participating and the people watching from the audience typically have an "aha" experience, as they come to realize that nothing the workers do can improve their performance. Until the task is redesigned with performance as its goal, no amount of effort by the worker or influence from the manager will improve the worker's performance.

For years, managers have incorrectly viewed people as the cause of poor work performance. Deming estimates that 80 percent of performance problems are attributable to organization and work-design issues — the misalignment of processes, structure, management systems, roles, tasks and resources — with only 20 percent attributable to worker issues. His work and the efforts to implement TQM in the workplace have had a remarkable impact in redirecting much of the performance-improvement effort in industry to the redesign of work. This redirection has in turn reduced the misuse of training as an intervention to improve performance.

The impact of work design on performance is clarified by viewing a company as a "whole system," as discussed briefly in Chapter 2. Based on Ludwig von Bertalanffy's *General System Theory*, an enterprise can be described as

- a whole system — a complete system that is made up of interdependent subsystems.
- an open system — a system that is dependent on the market environment in which it operates.

Viewing companies as *whole* and *open* systems helps to clarify the point Deming makes with his red beads. Individuals work within a larger system and carry out roles, perform tasks and use resources that are defined by and dependent on this larger system. In such a system, decisions and activities in which workers have no influence or control largely define the circumstances in which they work. As a result, workers have very limited opportunity to improve their performance . . . unless they are given some influence over the larger system.

This relationship is represented in **Figure 10.2** as a series of nested subsystems. If the reader will imagine being an individual worker performing a task in a company (in the oval in the middle of the drawing), and think of the ways that he or she might be dependent on the *work subsystem*, on the *organizational subsystem* and on the *strategic subsystem* of a company, this idea should become clearer yet. It is a helpful way to recognize the influence of work design, the organization and even corporate-level decisions on the individual worker's situation. It is precisely because of the strong influence of this hierarchy of subsystems that Deming makes it a practice to insist on (1) the CEO being part of the discussion and (2) "quality" being added to the corporate mission statement. He knows that unless focus and concern are given to "quality" as a *strategic* subsystem objective, efforts to achieve this goal in the *organizational* and *work* subsystems will fail.

These subsystems, and the elements within each, as listed in **Figure 10.3**, represent the *defining hierarchy* of a company's operations. Each subsystem in the hierarchy defines the context, or environment, for subsystems beneath it, just as each element in the hierarchy is defining for elements beneath it.* A brief review of each subsystem and element will clarify this point:

- *Strategic subsystem* - the design of this subsystem is the responsibility and focus of *senior executives*, and their work is to make defining decisions regarding philosophy, mission and strategy so as to establish a strategic context for decision-making and action within the organizational subsystem.
  - * *Philosophy* - provides a subtle yet powerful influence on every aspect of the enterprise; often established originally

---

* The exception to this rule occurs in companies that are smaller and more entrepreneurial. The hierarchy is more flexible in such companies, and it is not unusual to find a lower-level element defining the elements above. Take the case of a company with a unique resource, such as a gifted individual or valuable technology. Such a resource can easily become a defining factor for elements above it if the hierarchy is flexible. A more flexible company might redefine its mission, change its strategy, redefine its processes or make exceptions in its management systems if it identifies a unique capability among its employees. Well-established bureaucracies are generally too inflexible to capitalize on such a resource, and typically waste it — or run it off. Thus, uniquely capable employees leave bureaucracies to become defining elements for more flexible enterprises.

Figure 10.2
Organizations as Whole and Open Systems

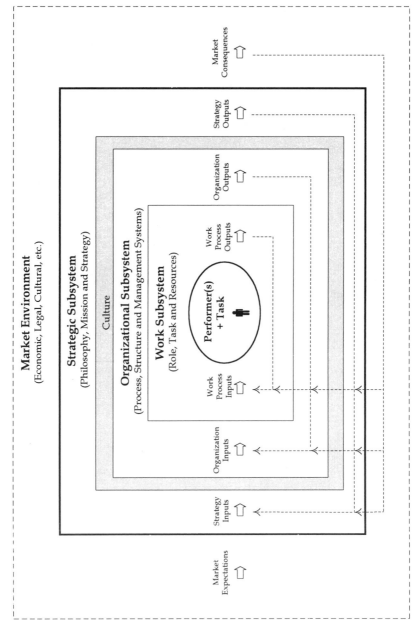

by the *founder* and then perpetuated with slight market-adaptive changes over time.

* *Mission* - serves as an umbrella for enterprise strategy, as in the selection of an industry and markets served.
* *Strategy* - consists of the major initiatives of the enterprise, and thereby determines organizational subsystem needs . . . particularly the principal processes that are necessary to accomplish the strategy.

* *Culture* - is somewhat of an anomaly in this hierarchy — though it is impacted by philosophy, mission and strategy, and has a similar capability to define the elements below it — because culture cannot be decided, selected and controlled *directly* as can the other elements; culture is the result of the environment (open system) and defining decisions made throughout the whole system, and is therefore subject to change only *indirectly*.

• *Organizational subsystem* - the design of this subsystem is the responsibility of *managers*, yet more recently has become the focus of *the entire organization at all levels*, and this work is to make defining decisions regarding processes, structure and management systems that (1) are in alignment with the context established by the strategic subsystem, and (2) establish an effective and efficient organizational context for decision-making and action within the work subsystem.
* *Process* - defines the strategic, core, support and administrative processes of the organization, thereby determining the appropriate organizational structure; processes are the focus of reengineering efforts, which explains why redesign invariably results in organizational *re*structuring.
* *Structure* - provides for the flow of responsibility, authority, information and decision-making within the organization to facilitate the effective and efficient operation of the processes.
* *Management systems* - are intended to reinforce the structure and support the processes of the organization to finely tune its operation; however, these systems are subject to control by self-serving prerogatives or innocent misuse; management systems have a defining influence on the

Figure 10.3
Hierarchy for the Design and Diagnosis of Enterprise Systems

Hierarchy #	Environmental Element	Issues Involved	System Level
1	Philosophy	Quality of life, meaning of work, ethics	
2	Mission	Organization purpose, goals, objectives, vision	Strategic Subsystem
3	Strategy	Planning, competitive initiatives, tactics, defined values	
4	Culture	Real values, customs, beliefs, norms	N/A*
5	Process	Macro-work design (reengineering), operations management, accountability	
6	Structure	Organization design, work units, hierarchy	Organizational Subsystem
7	Management Systems	Decision-making, recruiting, reporting, compensation	
8	Role/Job	Responsibilities, assignments, functions, relationships	
9	Task/Skill	Duties, activities, behaviors, attitudes, micro-work design (total quality)	Work Subsystem
10	Resource	Equipment, tools, people, technology, materials, schedules	

* Culture is a system output, not an input, and therefore not subject to design.

work subsystem, and are very often the cause of ineffectiveness and inefficiency in the work subsystem.

- **Work subsystem** - the design of this subsystem is the responsibility of *managers* and should be approached sociotechnically — with the workers designing the work to suit the available technology, and specifying the roles/jobs, tasks/skills and resources needed — yet it is more commonly approached as a nuisance task and delegated to Human Resources practitioners, industrial engineers or others. This work is to make defining decisions regarding the elements of work that (1) are in alignment with the context established by the organizational subsystem, and (2) have the capability to accomplish the specified work effectively and efficiently.
  * *Role/Job* - determines the process responsibilities and duties of individuals, consistent with the structure and management systems, and determines the needs for specific tasks/skills.
  * *Task/Skill* - defines the work of individuals and how the work will be performed, consistent with established roles/jobs and the management systems, and defines the resources that are required.
  * *Resource* - outlines the required resources — information, capital, equipment, materials, services, etc. — for accomplishing the tasks and fulfilling the roles of the organization; resources are frequently the last element to be determined, unless they are recognized beforehand to be a scarce resource, in which case they may need to be determined and assured as strategies or processes are defined.

This discussion equips the reader with a *systems perspective* — an essential tool for diagnosing and solving performance problems and for designing high-performance work. The whole-system hierarchy is presented in the PREPARE stage to draw attention to the extraordinary impact that strategic and organizational subsystems have on individual work performance. Note that the discussion of the PREDOMINATE and PRODUCE stages of the Humaneering process algorithm dealt with these same systems issues, but without specific reference to this hierarchy:

Stage	*System Level*
PREDOMINATE	Strategic Subsystem
PRODUCE	Organizational Subsystem
PERFORM	Work Subsystem

Combined, these three subsystems define the central decisions in any enterprise. Discussions of *system alignment*, perhaps unknowingly, are concerned with these elements and the rational argument that they should be "in alignment" — in proper relationship to each other. Performance improvement generally entails making interventions to adjust the system elements that are out of alignment.

Systems Approach to Improving Performance

The organizational and work subsystems directly influence individual work performance. The *organizational subsystem* establishes the context within which this work is performed, and the *work subsystem* controls the work itself.

As noted in Chapter 9, attempts to increase productivity invariably threaten or advance the performance of task-level work. This impact is due to the influence of the organizational subsystem — the focal point for efforts to increase productivity — on the work subsystem, and on roles and tasks in particular. This relationship makes it important to focus on reengineering (radical redesign) at the organizational level (processes) prior to redesign at the work level (tasks). Process improvements invariably alter roles and tasks, so oftentimes any prior efforts to improve tasks will become meaningless, because some tasks are ultimately eliminated or altered significantly through process reengineering.

Nonetheless, U.S. industry has primarily focused on quality (tasks) prior to reengineering (processes) because the initiative to improve quality originated 20 years earlier with industrial engineers who operate at the work subsystem level of companies. These engineers were not involved in process or strategy decisions at the time, and could not generate much interest in their concerns with senior managers or executives, so they focused on tasks — the area in which they could make a difference — even if it meant trying to work around organizational and strategic subsystems designed on completely different principles. Subsequently, TQM created a major breakthrough for this effort because it required CEOs and top executives to get involved.

Their involvement brought—or is in the process of bringing—the strategic and organizational subsystems into alignment with task-level quality improvements already underway. Once top management focuses on the requirements for competing in a global marketplace, emphasis then shifts to the reengineering of work at the process level. If management is not in tune with the needs for change at the organizational-subsystem (process) level, then industrious employees can only (a) *try to* get management's attention and support, (b) *try to* change the things they can control, (c) *try to* learn to live with a poorly designed work subsystem or (d) leave to find a company that wants to improve performance.

My rationale for presenting the Humaneering process algorithm in the order I have is probably easier to understand after this discussion. The design cycle begins with the PREDOMINATE stage because of the influence of the strategic subsystem on both organizational and work design. Without a corporate strategy to make the organization a competitive advantage, much of the work that must be done at the organizational and work levels will continually run up against a strategic subsystem with different priorities and policies.

Much of the focus in organizations today is on *improving performance*. With a systems perspective, we begin to better understand what changes might be needed to make these improvements. Many Training practitioners, influenced by the emphasis given to performance as the *goal of training activity* by NSPI, and more recently by the American Society of Training and Development (ASTD), are shifting the focus of their work to performance improvement. Some practitioners interpret this new focus as the need to follow through on training activity to assure that the knowledge and skills covered in training are successfully applied to the participants' work to effect the desired performance improvement. Others interpret this focus as an invitation into a new role within their organizations, working as "performance consultants" or "performance technologists" to improve performance wherever they can. Still others continue in their traditional roles as designers, developers or instructors.

Regardless of their direction, Training practitioners will be more effective in their work if they understand the elements involved in improving performance. If their role is shifted to consulting, then they will have to do considerable reading and gain relevant experience to understand the current technology related to the organizational and work subsystems, including organizational processes, structures, management systems, work roles, tasks and resources. Though space

Figure 10.4
Improving Organizational Subsystems

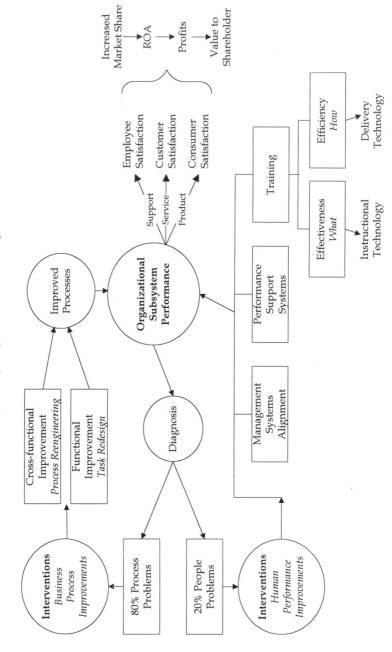

limitations restrict the depth to which this technology can be discussed here, **Figures 10.4** and **10.5** may provide a helpful orientation to some of the concerns in these areas.

The overall process for improving organizational subsystems is graphically represented in **Figure 10.4**. It begins with the *organizational subsystem performance* objective to provide *support, service* and *product* to satisfy *employees, customers* and *consumers*, respectively. This satisfaction—or delight, if it can possibly be achieved—ultimately translates into *value to the shareholder*. The improvement process itself begins with *diagnosis*, which *80 percent* of the time will indicate (thanks to Deming) the need for a *business-process* improvement intervention, which focuses on both process reengineering and task redesign, and results in improved processes. The remaining *20 percent* of the time, diagnosis will indicate the need for a *human-performance* improvement intervention.

Human-Performance Improvement Intervention

To make a human-performance improvement intervention, three alternative approaches should be considered, starting with the most effective and efficient and working toward the least. *Management systems alignment* entails the review and possible adjustment of one or more management systems that do not support the required performance. A *performance support system* could consist of a physical fixture, software program, directional signage, or other type of *job aid* that provides worker support (information, feedback, etc.) just at the moment it is needed, thereby alleviating the need to train workers and trust their memory and judgment. The last possible intervention is *training*, and it should be developed and delivered with maximum effectiveness and efficiency.

Improvement of the *work subsystem* should focus on the *role/job, task/skill* and *resource* elements—in that order. Because the task/skill and resource elements are discussed extensively in the TQM and "quality improvement" literature, the balance of this discussion focuses on the *role/job* element. **Figure 10.5** shows a hierarchy of requirements for the role/job element. This hierarchy outlines the *issues involved* in designing roles/jobs for high performance. These issues must be addressed and defined to support the desired result in order for the individual in the role or job to achieve high performance. Any issues out of alignment with the desired result will detract from the individual's

Figure 10.5
Hierarchy for the Design and Diagnosis of the
Role/Job Element in the Work Subsystem

Hierarchy #	Environmental Element	Issues Involved	Symptoms of Deficiencies
1	Explicit Role	Value-adding activity; organization and core-process alignment; operative work design; role-supporting relationships, systems, policies and procedures; and standards of performance	Under-utilization
2	Accountability and Empowerment	Responsibility; authenticity; trustworthiness; security; confidence; self-worth; rationality; respectability and respectfulness; flexibility; and helpfulness	Low self-confidence
3	Vision and Goals	Life purpose; principal values; positive attitude; focus and direction; and intrinsic motivation	Confusion
4	Necessary Capabilities	Relevant knowledge and understanding; helpful perspective; appropriate process and technical competence; and interpersonal skills	Anxiety
5	Meaningful Incentives	Potential for accomplishment (events), achievement (growth) and actualization (maturity); financial compensation and rewards (to satisfy security and discretionary needs); explicit recognition (to satisfy self-esteem needs); free time; fulfillment of individual needs; and extrinsic motivation	Limited effort
6	Adequate Resources	Authority; financial, physical and emotional support; time; leadership, guidance and feedback; and performance measurement	Frustration
7	Action Plan	Strategies, programs, projects and activities; timelines, schedules and deadlines; follow-up and evaluation	No follow-through
8	Development Plan	Assessment of strengths and weaknesses; self-directed learning; skill development; and performance improvement	Over-confidence

performance—generally in observable behaviors, noted in **Figure 10.5** as *symptoms of deficiencies.*

PBP developed this technology—based on substantial knowledge of the professional literature and exhaustive field research—initially to support our consultants with their performance-improvement work with clients, and more recently to prepare practitioners for internal performance-improvement consulting roles. It has endured considerable validation testing, and has proven itself through extensive use to be a reliable guide for design and redesign work. For *design*, the issues become a checklist to assure that every relevant issue has been considered and defined to support, not detract from, high performance. For *redesign*, the symptoms of deficiencies are a helpful tool for diagnosis, as it is often necessary to help the individual in the role/job to accurately determine what is missing or otherwise out of alignment. Efforts to improve individual performance should begin with the issues noted for the explicit role, and continue through the hierarchy. Issues identified as missing or out of alignment should be addressed in this same order. It will do little good to make changes to issues well into the hierarchy if the more fundamental issues in the first part of the hierarchy are omitted or out of alignment.

At this point, readers may feel overwhelmed as they come to realize all the work that needs to be done, and all the knowledge (technology) that needs to be acquired and integrated, for companies to support high-performance work in the years ahead. Yes, it is a big job . . . and this is a big reason why companies need the help of Training practitioners to meet this challenge. Top management knows that companies cannot succeed without these changes, and may not survive long enough if the changes are made one task, role or process at a time. They know that a complete *transformation* is required if they are to keep up with or get ahead of mounting global competition. The problem, though, is that too many people are defending the old ways of working—a response that is destined to put companies out of business and people in unemployment lines.

The High-Performance Work System

The best alternative for companies wanting to acquire and integrate the organizational technology to transform themselves may be the "high-performance work system" (HPWS) concept first discussed in Chapter 2. As noted in **Figure 10.6**, the HPWS may be the one approach that

Figure 10.6
Strategies to Improve Performance and Increase Productivity

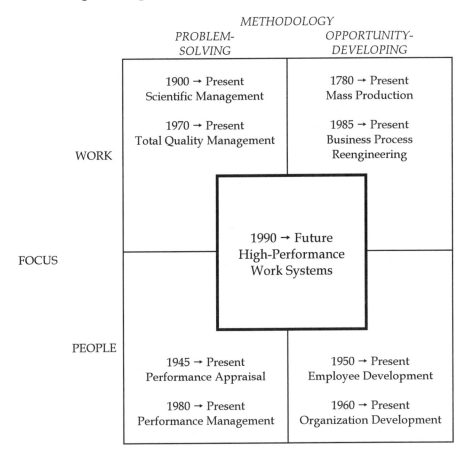

focuses on both work and people, as well as on problem-solving and opportunity development. It is a business formula that meets (1) *employers' needs* for ever-increasing performance and productivity from employees, and (2) *employees' needs* for an environment that provides effective performance support and facilitates their on-the-job learning and continuous performance improvement. Among the latest developments in the evolution of management principles and practices, the HPWS concept is an all-encompassing approach that integrates numerous important management innovations capable of improving the performance of today's companies. It incorporates the latest and best knowledge we have pertaining to the productive management of organizations.

The HPWS approach can also be described by reflecting on the principles for the design and management of organizations that it integrates. The design principles for an HPWS are outlined below:

1. *Market-driven design and operation*
   For a company to be successful, its design and activity must be driven by its customers and external environment. This characteristic enables groups of people working together to produce and deliver products and services that satisfy customers in a fast-changing marketplace.

2. *Empowered and self-managing teams*
   With exacting customer requirements to satisfy, groups with responsibility for complete products or entire markets, and with complete resource support, determine how best to do their work and manage themselves.

3. *Clear direction and expectations*
   Because work groups have a clear purpose, output requirements and agreed-on measures of performance, they can exercise great latitude in determining how their work will be done.

4. *Variance controlled at the source*
   Work groups and processes are designed so that errors can be detected and controlled where they occur, creating the need for proper information and tools to detect and prevent error.

5. *Integrated work systems*
   Human and technical systems are joint-optimized to create an integrated work system capable of responding to environmental and customer requirements and maximizing economic performance.

6. *Open access to information*
   Work groups require information (not just data) about the environment, process technologies, output, variances, etc., and have the ability to receive, apply, create and send information as needed.

7. *Flexible jobs and performance support*
   Individuals cross-train and share roles and responsibilities within work groups to broaden skills and knowledge, create flexibility, expand responsibility and participation, facilitate learning, and generate intrinsic motivation.

8. *Supportive human resource policies*
   Organizations adopt post-industrial employee treatment, including group-based selection, skill-based pay, performance support, peer feedback, team bonuses, minimum rank and hierarchy, and gain-sharing.

9. *Supportive management systems and culture*
   Executive sponsorship or internal design consistency assures the persistent support of management systems such as planning, budgeting, decision-making and information systems, and management processes.

10. *Capacity to redesign work processes*
    Work groups have the ability to improve or radically redesign their work processes as they determine the need to respond to environmental requirements and conditions.

With characteristics such as these, the HPWS approach has demonstrated extraordinary results in its almost 20 years of application. Nadler and Gerstein draw this conclusion:

> *Research and experience with HPWS have now yielded more than two decades of consistent evidence of the performance of units designed with HPWS principles as compared with those designed using traditional principles. In general, the data suggest that HPWS units produce the following results:*
> *Reduced costs . . . 40 to 50 percent less . . .*
> *Increased quality . . . consistent with total quality . . .*
> *Enhanced internal motivation . . . driven to do well . . .*
> *Lower turnover and absenteeism . . . commitment to the team . . .*
> *Increased learning . . . openness to new ideas . . .*
> *Increased capacity to adapt . . . respond to change more quickly* (1992).

Though the history of the HPWS concept includes successful applications by many well-known companies, its principles are not easy to implement and maintain. Some companies have performed significantly better than others, largely because of the way in which the new design approach was introduced. Adoption should be driven by the needs of the organization to enhance performance or to solve problems. It is clearly easier to implement the HPWS approach in a new organization than to redesign an existing work system, primarily because of the natural resistance to change. Change management and the necessary downtime for redesign need to be taken into account.

The HPWS approach is radically different from the design principles underlying the turn-of-the-century bureaucratic organization still in use by many companies. Though it may not be universally applicable, this concept is well suited to address two prevalent management challenges, both of which are at the center of the "training and development" dilemma. First is management's challenge concerning changes already made, or the need to make changes, to their organizations in response to dramatic changes in the market environment. The HPWS concept captures and integrates most of the organization-related improvements to the discipline of management in the past 50 years. Second is management's challenge to support a new and very different workforce of relatively sophisticated knowledge and service specialists. The HPWS concept provides helpful direction to management in creating an effective environment to support employees for maximum learning[2] and to effect significant improvements in performance and increases in productivity.

With an understanding of the basic principles of HPWS, Training practitioners and other organization members can think in these terms when considering organizational issues. Adoption of these principles will update and integrate Training's performance-oriented work within organizations.

Several texts describe this concept, though the terminology differs slightly. Three books that I frequently recommend include Marvin Weisbord's *Productive Workplaces* (Jossey-Bass, 1987), David Hanna's *Designing Organizations for High Performance* (Addison-Wesley, 1988) and David Nadler and Marc Gerstein's *Organizational Architecture* (Jossey-Bass, 1992). Furthermore, to Human Resources and Training practitioners who are interested in background reading on the human-resources development needs (their opportunity) in an HPWS, I recommend Malcolm Knowles' *The Adult Learner* (Gulf Publishing, 1990). With all the attention being paid to organizational performance during the past 40 years, there are also many other excellent books on the HPWS or its elements.

Whatever It Takes

Now let's return to the four questions posed at the start of this chapter to introduce the principal areas that challenge organizations which are trying to improve performance:

1. *Whose expectations?*
2. *What to measure?*
3. *What creates current results?*
4. *What will improve performance?*

It was suggested that the way these questions are answered has a major influence on the success of any enterprise. Too often, the answers are generated without full understanding of the subject and, as a result, performance is not improved, notwithstanding a considerable investment of time, effort and expense. If readers will study the material presented in this outline, and search out and study additional resources on the issues and concepts that were raised, they will be better prepared than almost anyone else in their organizations to diagnose the barriers to performance improvement and then to intervene wisely. They will also know the answers to those questions:

1.	*Whose expectations?*	Customers
2.	*What to measure?*	Customer delight
3.	*What creates current results?*	The whole system
4.	*What will improve performance?*	Probably not training

With these answers in mind, corporate Training practitioners could imagine that they may be out of business . . . all washed up. Nothing is further from my intended message. Rather, corporate Training needs to roll up its sleeves and get to work *with* management, and alongside organization members, doing whatever it takes to support the improvement of their performance. If Corporate training can apply its native talents to this end, it will be successful, and management will be satisfied — with fewer training classes this month than last. Performance is what matters.

11

Studying for Competence

stud · y · ing (stûd'e îng) v. 1. *To apply one's mind purposefully to the acquisition of knowledge or understanding of (a subject) as by reading, observation, or research <study a science>* 2. *To pursue a course of study.* 3. *To read carefully <study a text>.* 4. *To ponder: reflect.* 5. *To memorize.* 6. *To take (a course) at a school.*

Webster's New Riverside
University Dictionary (1988)

In 1973, David C. McClelland launched a great interest in "competency" as a better measure of capability and predictor of job success than intelligence, then the traditional measure. *Competency* is formally defined in this way:

> *A competency is an underlying characteristic of an individual that is causally related to criterion-referenced effective and/or superior performance in a job or situation* (Spencer and Spencer, 1993).

Since 1973, the associated concept of job or employee "competence" — *an individual's capacity to meet or exceed the minimum acceptable performance results* — has received considerable attention from researchers and practitioners alike. *Competence* relates specifically to an individual's capability to perform the work that is required, whereas *competency* relates to underlying characteristics that an individual possesses and is likely to use in any life role (Dubois, 1993). The expanded definitions below further clarify the difference between these terms:

> *Competency* - an *underlying characteristic* that is a deep and enduring part of a person's personality and is likely to predict behavior

in a wide range of situations (e.g., inherent motives, personality traits, natural skills, attitudes, and social roles), often referred to simply as "*stable traits*"

Competence - the *capability* to perform a task or role with acceptable results, to which an individual generally applies acquired knowledge, experience and skill—the result of "*task training*," education and practice—in combination with native competency

The rule for organizations to follow in regard to employees' competencies and competences can be expressed very succinctly:

- *Hire* for underlying characteristics (*competency*).
- *Assign* for performance capability (*competence*).

It is invaluable to an enterprise to know the *competencies* (underlying characteristics) that cause or actually predict who will do well or poorly in (1) the organization, (2) a significant role or job, and (3) a critical task or skill. Determining these competencies involves considerable additional effort. Whereas *task analysis* is a straightforward process for studying the attributes of a task or role, *competency analysis* is much more complex, because it is concerned *both* with *studying* the attributes of an organization, role or tasks, and *matching* them to the attributes of people. *With* knowledge of the indicated competencies, an organization can hire the most appropriate people with the greatest likelihood of success in specific roles. *Without* this knowledge, the enterprise and prospective employees both are seriously disadvantaged, particularly given the time and cost to hire, train and lose employees; and the importance of providing valuable services and the security of employment to individuals. There are resources readily available on the generic competencies indicated for many job categories, and though not precise to the company or a specific position, they are good starting points for generating more-specific knowledge about relevant competencies. There are also consulting firms that conduct the research necessary to customize this knowledge for an organization's needs.

Competencies, or *stable traits*, are a primary concern in the PICK stage of the Humaneering process algorithm. The goal is to identify and hire people on the basis of their stable traits, trying to make a match among the culture and environment of the organization, the roles and tasks, and the candidates, rather than to take a less-informed approach. Some more-sophisticated organizations have identified their "core" competencies—principal traits of employees that give organizations their distinctive advantages. Flexibility, high energy, project management, interpersonal skills, a need to serve and knowledge are all examples of core competencies. Many larger employers hire people primarily on how well applicants match these core competencies, particularly in the case of college recruiting efforts to fill entry-level positions in sales, production, programming or similar high-population roles, but in other situations as well. Companies that do not hire on this basis undoubtedly experience a much poorer "fit" of employees with their organization, and generally experience greater turnover and poorer performance as a result.

Competencies are also helpful in the PLACE stage. If the competencies of individuals are assessed as part of the hiring decision, it is particularly convenient to use this information again to place them in the "right" roles and specific jobs. However, more important when assigning people is their *role/task competence*—their *acquired performance capability* for that work. Since performance is the goal of all work, the capacity to perform becomes a principal criterion for assigning workers to specific roles or tasks. To the extent that workers are already capable, they do not require task training and are immediately available to perform their assigned work.

The PREPARE Stage

Individual capability at work is the focus of the PREPARE stage of the Humaneering process algorithm, and the goal is *employee competence*. (See **Figure 11.1**.) To achieve *employee competence* in a role or task requires (1) appropriate *stable traits*, (2) sufficient *acquired performance capability*, (3) focused *task training* that enables individuals to meet the minimum acceptable performance standards and (4) continuous *performance development*. The requirement for individuals to continually improve their *performance* at work (PERFORM stage) both demands and supports the parallel need for individuals to develop their *capability* at work.

The dynamic cycle of *performance development* that links capability to performance, and performance to capability, begins with individuals receiving task training that fully prepares them for minimum acceptable performance in new roles or tasks. For many roles and tasks that are very similar regardless of the organization in which they are

Figure 11.1
The PREPARE Stage
The Humaneering Process for Developing Organizational Competitive Advantage

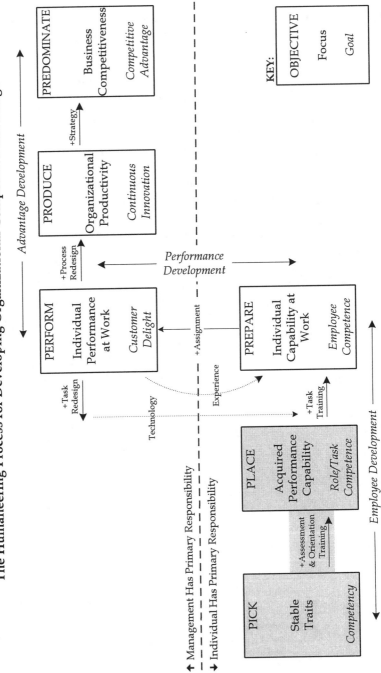

performed (as is often the case with professions and many other knowledge and service specialist roles), individuals are often fully prepared to perform following only an orientation to the new organization. If workers are not already sufficiently capable of performing minimum acceptable work, then management is generally inclined to provide resources to train them. Management is motivated to support this training because these workers will soon be the responsibility of managers, who *must* achieve high performance in order to delight customers. Because of their need to perform on the job, workers are naturally motivated to acquire the knowledge, skills and behaviors this performance will require. Once assigned to roles or tasks, workers *"cross the line"* into the PERFORM stage. In addition to the intrinsic and material rewards that workers receive for the value they add, they gain *experience* from successful *performance at work*—valuable experience that adds to their *employee competence.* And, through the continuous improvement of their work, they create new *technology,* which is then passed on to new workers in their initial *task training.*

The PREPARE stage emphasis on *individual capability at work* in turn establishes a context for the PLACE stage emphasis on *acquired performance capability,* stressing the need for workers to have role or task competence. The importance of *employee competence,* coupled with employees' responsibility for their own capability and its development, establishes among organization members a universal concern for learning and performance development.

Task Training

Notwithstanding the responsibility of workers to be capable of performing their roles or tasks, they may require task training to achieve, maintain or surpass minimum acceptable performance levels. Such training may be provided (1) by fellow workers or supervisors, (2) by staff trainers within the operations unit, (3) by the corporate Training function or (4) by outside training vendors. Task training is not the same as or a component of general development training. Research and experience have shown that development training is a poor investment of time and resources. It lacks value because it does not address the knowledge, skills and behavior required for specific work assignments.

Even workers who do not require task training will require some orientation to a new organization, department or unit. In most

Figure 11.2
Process Model for Adult Learning, Growth and Development

Stage	Description
Need	Learning and behavior change occur only when there is a strongly felt need to learn or change. This need may originate internally (e.g., self-image, goals, etc.) or externally (e.g., threat, reward, etc.).
Understand	The new knowledge or behavior must first be perceived, comprehended and accepted before it can be applied volitionally.
Practice	This knowledge or behavior must be used often, preferably in a safe and supportive environment closely relevant to its intended application.
Adapt	This knowledge or behavior must then be integrated with and adapted to the learner's natural behavior style.
Teach	The learner will encourage and coach others to use this same knowledge or behavior, thereby erasing all self-doubt about its effectiveness and value.

cases, new workers must learn the current methods, procedures, systems, etc., of the roles and tasks to which they have been assigned. They must also become acquainted with the unique characteristics of the work they will perform.

Since there is considerable literature on the subject of effective training, it is unnecessary to review it here . . . except for three issues that are both significant and frequently ignored:

- *Strongly felt need* - Learning occurs *only* when there is a strongly felt need to change, as in the case of skill development, behavior change and performance improvement. As a result, expectations of performance or performance improvement must precede any training activity for it to have relevance and be taken seriously. Therefore, it is inappropriate, and for that matter a virtual waste, to require training (mandated programs) or the use of training resources (spending two weeks in some form of training) unless an unequivocal requirement for action has been established preceding the training experience and enforced with consequences thereafter. (See **Figure 11.2**.)

- *Practice, adaptation and integration* - Performance development requires practice, adaptation and integration in order for learners to effectively enhance their established capabilities. (See **Figure 11.3**.) Therefore, for training initiatives to produce a change in employee capabilities (i.e., to have value), workers must be provided with a realistic simulation or on-the-job training experience, with coaching, to integrate their new knowledge with those capabilities. This is the only way to assure that workers can, in fact, effectively perform their roles or tasks. Absent these steps, workers will be unable to perform their assigned work to acceptable standards. It is important to remember that *performance capability* is the responsibility of the worker first and Training second . . . and potentially a problem for management.

  Therefore, Training practitioners, to fulfill their responsibility to management (Training's customer) and individual workers (Training's consumer), and to prepare employees for their work, must "cross the line" into management's domain — the workplace — and into the PERFORM stage of the Humaneering process algorithm. With performance on the job as the only legitimate goal for training activity, Training practitioners must understand the variables that impact performance and must be proficient in influencing these variables to achieve the desired result. Training's responsibility to support the continuous process of *performance development* also requires Training practitioners to "cross the line" into the workplace to provide this service effectively.

- *Scarce resources* - Cost-effectiveness and speed are essential elements of any support service provided to an economic enterprise . . . and training is no different from any other service in this regard. In virtually all cases, training designs do not reflect this priority in the spirit that management intends. As a result, most training programs are subject to "easy" redesign to (1) improve their impact and reliability for achieving the required results, (2) reduce their cycle time (from training need to final result), class time and time off the job, and (3) significantly reduce their cost. These changes can be accomplished through

Figure 11.3
Process Model for Adult Training

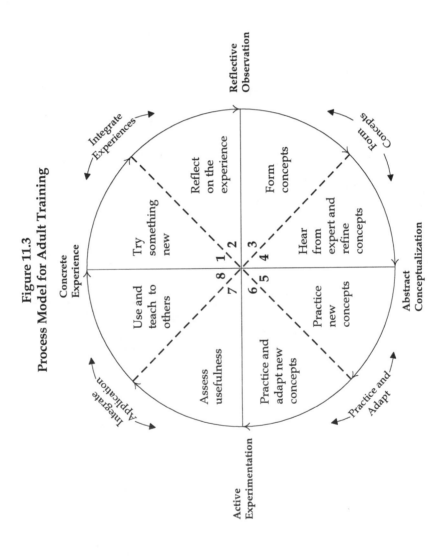

Adapted from Bernice McCarthy, *The 4MAT System: Teaching to Learning Styles with Right/Left Mode Techniques.* Barrington, IL: EXCEL, Inc., 1987.

a fast, systematic, straightforward process I developed years ago and named simply Training Redesign.

For the past few years, we have been teaching Training Redesign at public workshops and in house to more and more Training practitioners who recognize that they too have an obligation to continuously improve their work. PBP's Training Redesign process is previewed in Chapter 14, "Training — Better, Faster, Cheaper." Whether Training practitioners follow PBP's Training Redesign process, or develop their own, the opportunity looms large for Training to quickly add significant value by removing needless resources from current designs and better applying them to the many other pressing learning needs they can support.

Training initiatives have specific objectives, such as instructing workers on how to operate a machine or follow a certain procedure, and a goal of standardizing behavior. The reader is acquainted by now with another, very different learning need in organizations . . . a learning need that goes far beyond lectures, instructions, classrooms and other familiar aspects of bureaucratized behavior. This new learning need is inherent in the work of customer satisfaction, continuous improvement, process reengineering, self-directed teams, high-performance work systems (HPWS) and continuous performance development. It is learning^2 — the focus of the "learning^2 organization."

The question often arises, "How can the Training function support this new kind of learning — *learning^2*?" My answer to that question is typically something like, "Find a way . . . any way . . . to help people improve their performance. Don't teach, don't preach, and don't focus on anything else . . . just their performance. If you do that, they will appreciate you, their supervisor will appreciate you, and anybody else who cares about the performance of this organization will appreciate you. That's value-added."

Continuous Performance Development

Continuous performance development is a requirement for everyone in the workplace today . . . although, admittedly, some people are not yet aware of this new imperative. No longer is it true that having a skill and a clean job with a big company will provide security. Today, not even a college degree, management status and solid track record will guarantee a successful career. Markets, technology and priorities are so quick to change that the only security or assurance of success people have is their productive capabilities. "What value can you add today?" is the implicit rule. As a result, all employees must maintain their performance capability through performance-centered development.

Performance-centered development does not mean that workers will be expected to collect more continuing-education units (CEUs), attend more classes on teamwork or assertiveness, read *The Wall Street Journal* or the latest business text, or get an executive MBA . . . though performance-centered development might lead to any or all of these initiatives. Performance-centered development means that all organization members must apply themselves fully and continuously to the task of improving their performance. Competitive pressures demand it, and both management and organization members will expect no less. Self-directed study to improve performance will be expected of everyone. Not to do so is to risk functional obsolescence. In *Post-Capitalist Society*, Drucker confirms this threat:

> *Throughout history, craftspeople who had learned a trade had acquired everything they would ever need to know during their lifetime after five or six years of apprenticeship. In Post-Capitalist Society, it is safe to assume that anyone with any knowledge will have to acquire new knowledge every four or five years, or else become obsolete (1993).*

Many people let work define their lives. For some, performance is motivating because it confirms their self-concept . . . and supports their self-image. Other people are motivated to greater performance based on the security, recognition and material rewards that work provides. For them, work is a means to some other end. In this context, perhaps, we need to think of *achievement* or *pride* as affective competencies on which to base the hiring of employees—since these traits naturally motivate people to perform, to develop their performance capability and to improve their performance at work. Regardless of whether people are motivated intrinsically or extrinsically, we have come to know that *self-betterment*—the pivotal concept identified by Adam Smith—is the driving force for performance and performance development. This conclusion was summarized well by Charles R. Mann, Director of the American Council on Education, in the *Journal of Adult Education*, February 1929:

The American people seem to realize that their greatest material success depends upon the degree to which each worker finds the right opportunity for self-education on the job.

Michael McGill and John Slocum, professors of organizational behavior at Southern Methodist University, draw a similar conclusion in their recent book, *The Smarter Organization*:

Learning is its own reward. In a smart organization, the value of learning is constantly reinforced by managers and other employees. Workers know from every experience with the organization that learning is significant. Because learning profits the individual as well as the organization, workers feel a sense of personal connection to their own learning agenda. Learning allows workers to influence what and how they learn; they are autonomous learners. Finally, learning provides continuous feedback while always advancing the learning target. The sense of competence that individuals derive from learning is at once the most valuable reward and the most effective motivator to further learning (1994).

The motivation for learning, improvement and performance development is inherent in all people. It may not have been supported in childhood, or it may have been distorted by a bureaucratized educational system, but it is there. The challenge for the Training function is not to motivate people to learn. Rather, Training's challenge is to support performance development and the development of employee competence. Meeting this challenge may entail diagnosing needs for improvement, constructing performance models, facilitating performance-development contracts, supporting quality improvement and reengineering, or helping management transform the enterprise into a high-performance work system. This is the *"new work"* of corporate Training.

Part IV

Training Gets to Work

I see a drastically new role evolving for the human resource developer as we begin to conceptualize an organization as a system of learning resources. The role of human resource developers then becomes that of manager of these systems — quite a different role from that of the past, as manager of the logistics of operating training programs of courses, workshops, seminars, and other scheduled activities.

Malcolm S. Knowles
The Adult Learner (1990)

The potential for Training to contribute to the enterprise and its organization members has never been greater or more important than it is today. Human performance will become the most important variable for management, and newly found effectiveness in improving it will quickly earn the respect and support of management. However, to realize this potential, a transformation of the Training function is required so that its work can be conducted in the context of performance improvement. This is Training's opportunity . . . to expand its role and strategic influence. The transformation is from *training resource* to *source of competitive advantage*.

The Need to Add Value

The challenges of managing a business today exceed what we could only have imagined a few years ago. It is vital for Training to understand and appreciate management's role and responsibility, and to support it in any way possible. These possibilities range from improving human performance, to establishing a competitive advantage in the marketplace, to simply making more productive use of time and budgets. These are everyone's responsibilities.

The major paradox in business today is that everyone is expected to do more (i.e., to add more value), do it better, faster, and cheaper, and do it with fewer resources. This kind of pressure can create or exacerbate a *we/they* division between Training practitioners and management . . . unless it is realized and accepted that these are the realities of business at this time! All the more reason for Training to pursue and develop as much understanding of the business as they possibly can, and to continuously propose and launch training and performance-improvement initiatives that support business goals and improve business performance. The key is to add value, and to be able to show that it has been added, using whatever means are available and accepted.

The Short Answer and the Long Question

Let us shift our attention to what's possible, and go beyond the typical boundaries of a traditional Training function. Recent research has established two crucial facts: (1) that organizational factors (i.e., people, communication flow, decision-making practices, job design, goal emphasis, etc.) contribute about twice as much to profit rates as economic factors (i.e., industry profitability, market share, total assets, etc.); and (2) that organizational competencies are likely the *only* potential source of *sustainable* competitive advantage. What can we do with this information?

Undoubtedly, corporate Training departments have many options. Then again, do they? The answer depends on the situation in which departments find themselves, in terms of industry environment, corporate focus, organizational resources, management support, department leadership, etc. — the list goes on and on.

Because I cannot possibly know readers' situations, I will offer two proposals, in the hope that one or the other, or something in between, contains some nuggets of helpful advice. The first proposal is simply a to-do list of suggestions that will bring corporate Training closer to alignment with management. The second proposal outlines a more comprehensive strategy to transform the corporate Training function into its organization's source of competitive advantage. They begin with the same premise: that corporate Training departments need to increase their value-added to their organizations.

Greater Alignment with Management

Certainly, some of the traditional corporate Training and Human Resource Development activity is both helpful and effective in generating value-added, short or long term. To expand on this base, corporate Training must seek greater *alignment with management* by implementing any or all of the following suggestions:

- Recognize that if the contribution to a business goal is not clear, then the activity is probably optional.

- Keep up with corporate strategy.

- Appreciate that management has its reasons. As Covey says, *"Seek first to understand, then to be understood."*

- Know what you can do to improve human performance.

- Expend resources in ways that make money.

- Concentrate on doing everything better, faster, and cheaper — that is, if you need to do it at all.

- Make needs analysis by having short talks, not distributing long surveys.

- Find out what's #1 on management's hit list, and do something to help.

- Minimize training activities to the essential.

- Choose efficient instructional designs . . . that means cheap and fast.

- Try mentoring — the cheapest form of training — because everybody wins.

- Remember, people who need to know or do something will figure it out on their own if you can't make it easier for them.

- Cross-train your staff to multiply your effectiveness without increasing your expenses.

- Target the resource-intensive training programs and redesign them to 50 percent of the present time and cost.

- Centralize development and de-centralize delivery.

- Use homemade video for distant instruction.

- Evaluate all interventions up to Kirkpatrick's *Level 4* (i.e., performance on the job), and let your customers and others know about the impact you're having.

- Be reactive . . . and be quick about it.

- Make plans, but don't be a slave to them.

- Be prepared to change initiatives quickly.

- Focus on creating materials, not on stand-up instruction.

Readers might be interested to know that the above list of suggestions was *produced by a client*—a group of corporate Training practitioners—with whom I have had the pleasure to work for several months. Although the list sounds much like my ideas, I believe it expresses their genuine encouragement for others to make the same kind of constructive changes they are making.

From Resource to Source of Competitive Advantage

Since much more can be done to advance human performance in organizations, and because no unit of the organization is better grounded in the human-performance technology that is central to achieving this potential, Training leadership is compelled to launch a major strategic initiative to this end. Such a radical goal will undoubtedly lead to the restructuring of the Training function—rethinking and redefining its purpose, redesigning and reengineering its processes, and repositioning and redeploying its resources within the organizational structure—

to lead the way for complementary support functions to join in this effort. This initiative represents extraordinary potential for organizations, and a more credible professional role for corporate Training.

To complete such a restructuring is hard work for an organization, and not a strategy to be undertaken capriciously. A business case is needed to warrant such bold action, and the payoff needs to hold great promise for the organization—for management, for employees and for Training practitioners—if it is to be successful. Training leadership must be concerned first with understanding the factors and forces that are present in their organizations, and in their organizations' business environments.

Training practitioners could ask themselves this question: How should a corporate Training function be organized, both internally and relative to its external environment, in order that the services it provides will have the greatest usefulness for operating managers in improving the human performance of their organizations? Quick answers to the question would likely restate current decisions, indicating that, for the most part, Training practitioners still do not understand the question, the situation, the alternatives and the reasons why other alternatives might have greater value.

Alternatively, Training practitioners could determine what corporate Training services currently provide the greatest value to their organizations, the problems and opportunities that operating managers deal with, the ways in which training and other interventions might be useful in making these more manageable, and the methods required to provide those services. Thorough observation and group-process analysis would point to a pattern of needs and corresponding services, supplying some of the necessary criteria for making decisions.

Notwithstanding the temptation to trust current perceptions and instincts, the central challenge in organizational redesign is integrating information from (1) the environment that defines the requirements for services in the context of their application and intended result, and (2) the relevant technologies that underlie the dynamics of the situation under consideration. The object of this process is to develop a clear and realistic picture of the situations and goals which the department is going to support. With this picture clearly in focus, organization members can design strategies that contribute significantly to the accomplishment of their goals. Of course, to do so, one needs an understanding of the significant forces germane to meeting the needs of a particular organization, and the discipline to ignore the irrelevant.

Figure IV.1
A Four-Phase Transformation
From Training Resource to Source of Competitive Advantage

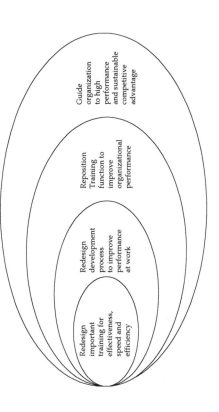

Phase	Objective	Approach	Timing
#1	Provide world-class instruction.	Redesign important training programs.	3 to 6 months
#2	Improve human performance at work.	Redesign development process.	6 to 12 months
#3	Improve organizational performance.	Reposition Training function.	1 to 3 years
#4	Establish organizational competitive advantage.	Guide organization to high performance.	3 to 5 years

Absent that specific knowledge, but having been at this point of discussion many times before, I can offer the following plan—a *roadmap* for restructuring the Training function.

This plan has four phases that together will require, on average, a three-to-five-year commitment to accomplish. Refer to **Figure IV.1** for a snapshot of this four-phase transformation—from training resource to source of competitive advantage. The following outline summarizes the key initiatives, each playing a central role in the transformation. This is a "bottom-up" strategy. (Note the reference to system levels and elements in parentheses. Refer to Chapter 10 and see Figure 10.3 for further definition.)

A premise upon which this plan is based is that the relationship between management and corporate Training can best be described as "between neutral and very negative." A more positive relationship could advance the process considerably.

1. *Provide world-class instruction* (Work).
   Talk is cheap and management has heard enough promises—action is the only effort with credibility. Therefore, this plan begins with activities that are well within corporate Training departments' operating authority. Emphasize enhancing credibility and strengthening corporate Training's relationship with its clients by showing a higher degree of alignment with management, a serious focus on improving performance and a reduction of waste. Behind the scenes, concentrate on acquiring advanced technology and skills relevant to performance improvement.

   - *Demonstrate alignment* (Task/Resource) - take the initiative to redesign important, resource-intensive training programs for greater effect, speed and efficiency. (See Chapter 14, "Training—Better, Faster, Cheaper," for details about Training Redesign.)

   - *Strengthen client relationships* (Role/Task) - learn how to work together with clients, showing empathy, openness and support in addressing, and in potentially meeting, clients' stated needs, wants and desires.

   - *Support performance goals* (Role/Task/Resource) - focus on clients' performance goals and use every available resource to deliver performance improvement as the result of these interventions.

2. *Improve human performance at work* (Work).
Now working from positions of increased credibility, yet no greater formal authority, fully exploit corporate Training's capabilities to have the greatest possible impact in improving the performance of individuals and work groups.

- *Function as internal consultants* (Role) - begin to act and work as consultants to all organization members.

- *Intervene beyond training* (Task) - provide "whole systems" interventions to remove performance barriers wherever possible . . . making training programs the last alternative considered.

- *Produce performance support* (Resource) - enlist the support of the other staff support functions to provide permanent solutions to performance problems.

3. *Improve organizational performance* (Organization).
Having demonstrated the capability to work in the role of con-sultants — with the cooperative support of other staff support functions — and to effect the improvement of performance, now propose the fundamental restructuring of corporate Training to make permanent a new role as a *Performance Improvement unit* that operates cross-functionally with the leadership of the prior corporate Training department. The significance of this re-structuring cannot be overstated. The *Convergence Strategy*, as clients have named it, calls for the operational merging of all functions providing staff support to a company's newly formal-ized performance improvement process (e.g., Training, Human Resources Development, Organization Development, Informa-tion Systems, Facilities, Recruiting, Industrial Engineering, etc.). Working as a matrixed organization, each function would retain its functional orientation for technology management and professional development purposes, yet more important, each function will assign staff members to cross-functional teams responsible and accountable to facilitate the improve-ment of performance at targeted areas of opportunity within

the core, strategic and administrative processes of an enterprise. This restructuring will be essential if companies are to
tear down the structural barriers that inhibit the cooperation of
these functions—cooperation that is essential if the goal is to
make effective process interventions. It has proven to be an
extraordinarily helpful strategy to eliminate myopic and self-
serving staff work. This strategy is necessary to maximize the
potential for performance improvement.

- *Practice continuous improvement* (Process) - assume
  responsibility for facilitating and supporting the organization's need to practice continuous improvement.

- *Converge support resources* (Structure) - assume leadership
  of the new cross-functional unit.

- *Facilitate a learning[2] climate* (Management Systems) -
  assume responsibility for supporting an environment for
  organizational learning[2].

4. *Establish organizational competitive advantage* (Strategy).
   Now, with the responsibility and cross-functional resources
   within reach, take the strategic role of guiding the organization
   to the development of human performance in core process
   areas where competitive advantage can be achieved.

   - *Propose options for competitive advantage* (Strategy) -
     identify areas of mediocre   human performance where
     significant increases in performance have the potential to
     establish competitive advantage, and recommend these to
     management for development.

   - *Demonstrate acumen and proficiency* (Strategy) - focus the
     full skill and knowledge of the unit's members on this
     opportunity.

   - *Innovate powerful interventions* (Strategy) - design,
     develop and deliver interventions that are fully capable of
     improving performance to target levels.

Regardless of the road chosen, the future will ask of Training practitioners that they accept greater responsibility, act with greater accountability and perform with greater proficiency.

Performance Improvement Unit — Roles, Goals and Responsibilities

The opportunity to generate highly capable organizations begs for a potent response from corporate Training and Human Resource Development practitioners. This response may include initiatives that span a wide range, from a tactical to-do list to a strategy that seeks to achieve a competitive advantage. In order to develop the high performance that is inherent in human resources, these practitioners must adopt the following roles, goals and objectives:

- *Developer of Effective Human Performance*
  Goal - Effectiveness
  Objectives:
    * Responsibility for human performance at all levels
    * Commitment to demonstrable results
    * Accountability to management

- *Trustee to Manage Training/HRD Investments*
  Goal - Efficiency
  Objectives:
    * Quick response to client problems
    * Short cycle time to complete interventions
    * Discernment of investments in interventions for performance improvement
    * Conservative management of financial resources

- *Producer of Effective Human Performance Interventions*
  Goal - Competence
  Objectives:
    * Consultative support of clients
    * Complete interventions, from analysis to evaluation
    * Targeting of all relevant context levels for intervention
    * Use of effective and efficient intervention methods

By recognizing their responsibility and adopting this strategy, corporate Training practitioners will (1) best serve their organizations' needs, (2) earn the respect and trust of executive and line management, and (3) secure the credibility and value-added of corporate Training.

Technology Transfer

One of the principal reasons for writing this book was to use the most cost-effective method of *technology transfer* — the written word — to introduce readers to solutions for problems that organizations now face and that the Training function has the potential to solve. It is naive, however, to think that all the answers can be provided within the covers of a single book. Some individuals will find in *Future Training* all they need to begin the journey of transformation. For others, the ideas and solutions introduced here may entice them to learn more. For them, we routinely provide public and in-house briefings or workshops on many of the subjects covered herein.

Clients that have started this journey have pointed out to me two fascinating conclusions that are not otherwise reflected in this strategy. First, it may be hard work and may require going back to school (figuratively), but it is probably the most exciting time ever in their careers. Second, the process does not flow in neat steps, one after the other, and it never ends — there is always more that can be done to improve one aspect or another of a situation.

Tools for Corporate Training's New Work

A number of "tools for improvement" are briefly introduced in Part IV. In Chapter 12, "Appreciative Inquiry," I introduce a sophisticated method for planning and action that emphasizes and builds on an organization's strengths. Chapter 13, "Performance Development," discusses the need to restructure Training initiatives to focus on performance development. In a radical departure from current practices, learners must be perceived as adults who are ultimately responsible for their own learning. Chapter 14, "Training — Better, Faster, Cheaper," introduces the Training Redesign concept, a systematic process developed by PBP to improve the effectiveness and efficiency of training. And finally, Chapter 15, "Internal Consulting," outlines PBP's Process Guide to Internal Consulting for Performance Improvement. This process stresses an action-research approach to developing high-performance work systems.

12

Appreciative Inquiry

What we ask determines what we find.
What we find determines how we talk.
How we talk determines how we imagine together.
How we imagine together determines what we achieve.
                    David L. Cooperrider, Ph.D.
                    Case Western Reserve University

We have grown accustomed to a problem-solving approach to life and work. If there were no problems, we would have nothing that we just *had* to do. But since there are plenty of problems when we look for them, we really never finish. It is always possible to spot a deficiency if we are willing to expect just a bit more than we see. So it happens that we sow our creative thoughts and abilities in tending our garden of problems.

We hear that the corporate world around us is in a state of "permanent whitewater," and we know the environment to be so chaotic that it is difficult for thinking people to decide where they are and where they want to go. Instincts tell us to defend and protect all that we do and know as right, and our sensibility follows along behind. But why? That's simple. Because others come to attack, to criticize and to declare us wrong and without value. It is only our human nature . . . and it is a good trait to have.

But what happens, when what we do and know IS wrong . . . or at least not as right as it once surely was? Can we trust enough to listen? Can we be sure? We would perhaps like to, but probably not. Better to trust our instincts.

And so the cycle continues, with no way to stop it for a positive thought. This experience may be all too much like that of Training practitioners. Everywhere they turn, in everything they read, everybody is trying to fix them. "Do this. Do that. Whatever you do, don't do . . . ."

Notwithstanding my decidedly optimistic view of the Training function, I have been accused on occasion of sounding negative as I discuss the issues that now threaten its future. Such accusations disturb me, because I know that when people hear "negatives," their learning stops, their defenses go up, and nothing generative can develop.

However, as I make presentations, even as I write this book, there are situations in which I feel compelled to get your attention, to help you reframe your view so that you are not caught defenseless. Once I have your attention, then I can teach what you may not see or know.

Working with clients is a different situation altogether. They see their problems, or at least the symptoms; so my role may be to examine a situation, gather more information, feed back what I see, search for causes, imagine alternatives and help construct a case for change. That work, too, can be focused on problem-solving. But once it is time to move forward with people, that is the time to take a positive approach — with appreciative inquiry (AI).

As the name implies, AI is a search for that which is appreciated. In business, "what is appreciated" translates to value-adding, productive, useful, effective and helpful. Because of its positive focus, AI has unique capabilities to stimulate constructive organizational change and to discover, understand, and foster innovation. A sophisticated method of examination, analysis and evaluation for planning and action, it is the preferred choice of PBP for all of our assessment work with clients, particularly when the focus is Training, OD, HR and other staff services. In adopting this approach, we knew that if we could help people see the effective and value-adding things they were doing, and help them focus on and channel their efforts into creating even more of these same value-adding results — the client would soon look for things to *quit* doing in order to free resources for more of what works.

The focus throughout the AI process stresses the positive:

- Increasing value-added to organizations
- The energizing strengths of the department
- An appreciation for current reality
- A positive future based on current reality

Appreciative Inquiry Process

The basic four-step process for AI is strikingly different from conventional models of analysis and problem-solving. These usually involve the assessment of the problem, analysis of the causes, consideration of alternatives and the development and implementation of an action plan. The AI approach is more like a positive, action-research intervention, which is evident from the process steps:

- *Discovering* - through reflection on the department's history and an exploratory discussion of work that has created the greatest value for the organization, zero in on the factors and forces that created the possibility for them.

- *Envisioning* - when the best is identified and valued, a natural reaction is to see a positive future based on more of the same.

- *Dialoguing* - through the open discussion of this future and the factors and forces that will make it a reality, a consensus emerges whereby people form a collective appreciation — a shared vision — of the future.

- *Co-creating* - having preserved the positive energy of the department and channeled it consensually toward a collective view of the future, department members find innovative ways, grounded in reality, to make the future a reality.

One result of the AI process is that problems are "left behind" rather than attacked and solved directly. This approach allows departments to eliminate their problems, yet do so without continually focusing on what does not work, generally a de-motivating experience for most people. PBP instead leads participants to capitalize on the energizing strengths of their departments, emphasize ways of increasing value-added for their organizations, appreciate their current reality, and envision a positive future based on current reality. Remarkably, this process works equally well with a variety of groups, such as Training departments, production workers and senior management groups.

The results are impressive. The AI process consistently yields positive, performance-developing direction to groups that follow the process. Perhaps even more important than this positive direction, the

AI process energizes . . . rather than de-energizes . . . participating groups, as do conventional problem-solving approaches. If there is a secret to performance development, then keeping people positive and thereby energized has to be that secret.

By now you know that I see a BIG future for corporate Training. Not because Training people are great people—some of the greatest—but because there is an extraordinary job to be done in our organizations if they are to remain viable and to become vibrant entities. The people in the best position to do this job are Training practitioners. And to lead corporate Training in this direction, they need to be value-adding, to see the need to rethink their role and methods, to map out a new position in organizations, to volunteer for significant changes to their routines, to learn much broader capabilities, to work with an organizations that are increasingly cynical about management and training, and to lead the organization to a competitive advantage. That is a BIG job, and it will require that Training practitioners remain positive and energized, so they can be *value-adding, productive, useful, effective and helpful.*

We recommend AI to our clients. We use AI as the framework for guiding corporate Training clients to their place in the future. And we teach the AI technology in-house to practitioners who are seeking a positive approach to interventions for managed change.

13

Performance Development

If evaluated by the number of training programs run, American industry is doing a splendid job of training its employees! However, if the real purpose of training is to "produce competent performers," employees who can perform their jobs more effectively (and efficiently) than they could before the training, then we are not doing as well. Our training interventions are seldom powerful enough to develop sufficient competence and confidence to transfer to truly effective on-the-job performance.

Dean R. Spitzer
"Training for Competence"
Educational Technology (1993)

According to Malcolm Knowles, most of the elements of adult learning theory had been discovered by 1940, but it remained for great minds working in various disciplines of the human sciences to clarify, elaborate on and refine this knowledge. Scholars like Abraham Maslow, Carl Rogers, Gordon Allport, Cyril Houle, Allen Tough and Knowles himself subsequently unified this knowledge into a contemporary theory of adult learning—andragogy. In a similar way and time, accepted principles of teaching emerged from scholars like Edward Thorndike, Ivan Pavlov, John Dewey, B. F. Skinner, N. L. Gage, Kurt Lewin, Robert Gagne and many others (1990). The integration of these developments in learning and teaching provide us with the best direction for the development of employees.

Andragogy (adult learning theory) is a radical departure from *pedagogy*—the art and science of teaching children—the basis for American school education and most corporate training. It is grounded in the premise that people mature naturally as they become adults and decrease their dependency on their parents and other adults. Both andragogy and pedagogy make underlying assumptions based on where the learner is in this maturation process:

- *Andragogy* - assumes the learner is an *adult*, and therefore independent, responsible and self-directing
- *Pedagogy* - assumes the learner is a *child*, and therefore dependent, irresponsible and incapable of self-direction

If we think of adults and children—at their most mature and their least mature, respectively—as opposite ends of a continuum, then we can imagine that, with regard to maturity, all people fit somewhere in between:

Least   **Most**
Mature • ————————————————————————→ • **Mature**
(child)   *Natural maturation process*   *(adult)*

Natural maturation is simply a decrease in dependency that occurs as people age. Andragogical theory asserts that, as this maturation process occurs—as people progressively give up their dependency, accept responsibility for themselves and become self-directed—the most appropriate instructional methods and learning environment for people should shift accordingly. According to Knowles, a continuation of pedagogical methods

> is practiced increasingly inappropriately [as people mature]. *The problem is that the culture does not nurture the development of the abilities required for self-direction, while the need to be increasingly self-directing continues to develop organically. The result is a growing gap between the need and the ability to be self-directing, and this produces tension, resistance, resentment, and often rebellion in the individual* (1990).

At first, it might sound ludicrous to management that corporate Training would design programs to train employees as though they were children, yet the underlying rationale closely parallels management's selection of bureaucracy for its organizational structure. Bureaucracy and pedagogy are based on similar assumptions. Note this parallel in the following two descriptions of the treatment of *employees/learners* by *managers/teachers*:

- *Employees/learners have dependent self-concepts* - managers/teachers consider employees/learners dependent personalities; therefore, employees'/learners' self-concepts are, or eventually become, dependent.
- *Managers/teachers know best* - employees/learners do not know what is important or the one right way to do things; therefore, managers/teachers have to control what employees/learners know and do not know and assume that employees/learners will not work/learn unless threatened with bad evaluations/grades.

In both cases, employees and learners are viewed as though they are children rather than mature adults. Accordingly, they are put in environments and treated in ways that reinforce this perception — ultimately motivating the employees/learners to adapt to the situation (i.e., the authority and control of the managers/teachers) as dependents.

A comprehensive comparison of the parallel between theories of learning/teaching and theories of organization/management is offered in **Figure 13.1**. The guiding principles that organizations need to heed are straightforward:

1. *Align learning strategy with organizational design* - congruence with organizational design should be the basis for selecting either pedagogical or andragogical theories for learning, change, employee development and performance-improvement strategies.
2. *Design learning interventions for specific situations* - congruence with specific situations should be the basis for selecting either pedagogical or andragogical theories for individual interventions for learning, change, employee development or performance improvement.

The implications of these principles for corporate Training functions are significant, depending on the extent to which (1) organizations utilize, and want to continue utilizing, bureaucratic organizational designs and (2) corporate Training has updated its practices for post-industrial organization design. These principles suggest that traditional training might well be appropriate for (1) standardization training, much like that which professionals require to learn the basic

Figure 13.1
A Comparison of Pedagogy and Andragogy:
Assumptions, Applications and Intervention Design

Topic	Pedagogy (child learning theory)	Andragogy (adult learning theory)
Assumptions		
Learners/employees	Dependent	Independent
Subject matter	One right way	Many ways
Motivation to learn, change or improve	External Dictated by others	Internal Response to personal/ career needs
Role of experience	Unimportant	Basis for learning, change or improvement Must integrate Rich resource
Learner/employee self-concept	Need direction	Capable of self-direction
Learning orientation	Subject-centered Logic-oriented	Life/career-centered Process-oriented
Objective	Minimum requirements	Self-betterment
Applications		
View of human nature	Theory X	Theory Y
Nature of work	Necessary evil	Vehicle for self- expression
Organization design	Bureaucracy	High-Performance Work System (HPWS)
Organization goals	Stable, slow-changing, highly structured performance	Dynamic, fast-changing, continuous improvement
Organization climate	Authority-oriented Formal/closed Competitive	Respect-oriented Informal/open Collaborative

Figure 13.1 (continued)
A Comparison of Pedagogy and Andragogy:
Assumptions, Applications and Intervention Design

Topic	Pedagogy (child learning theory)	Andragogy (adult learning theory)
Applications (continued)		
Diagnosis of needs	Supervisor	Mutual/self-diagnosis
Purpose of intervention	Orientation Standardization Learning	Change Development Learning[2]
Employee competence	Below minimum acceptable performance	Above minimum acceptable performance
Intervention Design		
Establishes need	Mandate	Performance improvement expectation
Intervention	Training	Facilitated experience
Process	Instruction, memorization, modeling, demonstration and coaching	Experience, new information, interpretation, practice, adaptation and integration

knowledge and methods of their work, or (2) initial orientation and indoctrination of workers to new roles or tasks. However, this training will be expected to lead directly to performance on the job, and to require a minimum of time and expense—a significant change in itself. Beyond these applications for traditional training, however, current training approaches will be out of alignment for organizations that are—or are being transformed into—high-performing operations.

To move to more-andragogical intervention designs, many Training practitioners will need to unlearn many of the instructional concepts and practices that they have used for years. They will need a better understanding of *training* and of *development*, and the differences between these two very different interventions. Training teaches facts and procedures; it standardizes and bureaucratizes, effectively

Figure 13.2
Five Phases of Human-Performance Development

Phase	Level*	Objective	Focus	Methodology	Evaluation
Fifth	N/A	Learning[2]	Create <u>new</u> knowledge through application of expert knowledge to create results.	Professional expertise applied with openness, trust, rational thinking and creative problem-solving	Demonstrated insight, ideas and innovation, with 360° validation and periodic re-validation
Fourth	N/A	Competence	Achieve capability to perform when and as needed (i.e., repeated performance, mastery, professional expertise).	Deliberate application of personal strengths and development of complementary behaviors	Demonstrated performance in varied circumstances, with 360° validation and periodic re-validation
Third	#4	Performance	Improve human performance (i.e., task competence).	Performance systems design, utilizing all means relevant to performance	Measured improved performance in target metric
Second	#3	Behavior	Change behavior as required.	Systemic training design, recognizing behavior as environmental adaptation	Measured change in behavior
First	#2	Instruction	Acquire knowledge, skill and/or attitude.	Enhanced instructional systems design, fully utilizing instructional, cognitive, psychological and behavioral sciences	Satisfactory examination score
N/A	#1	Attendance (i.e., customer attitude)	Participate as required.	Instructional systems design, with emphasis on entertainment	Positive participant reaction

* The Four Levels of Evaluation were originally profiled by Donald L. Kirkpatrick in 1959.

inhibiting development.   It teaches that there is "one best way" to work—a concept potentially inconsistent with learning[2], continuous improvement, adult behavior and diversity.   Training has its place; however, it is clearly over-specified as an intervention in organizations.

Development, by contrast, occurs naturally for adults who are challenged, supported and free to innovate. The key to development is focus—then safety, then support. Every executive, manager and employee desperately needs a performance-centered development plan. Not theoretical learning . . . that employees can get on their own if they are interested . . . but learning[2] that pays for itself in performance improvement. When employees improve their performance, they increase their competence, and with competence, their upward mobility. *Performance-centered development* is the most practical way to increase employee capability on the job; it improves employee performance—the only predictable path to increased rewards from work, and the only way to equitably repay the stakeholders for their investment.

General development training, potentially the largest single focus of corporate Training activity, needs to become a practice of the past—replaced by *performance-centered development*. To make this shift, Training practitioners will have to (1) change the *expectations* of management and employees, (2) change the *methods* of evaluation that promote entertainment over performance, and (3) endure the *initial disapproval* of employees—a common occurrence as people adjust to the new experience of being treated as adults at work. **Figure 13.2** outlines the five phases of human-performance development. Corporate training will have to innovate new ways to support this natural progression of learning and change. Independent, self-directed learning methods and formative feedback will become top priorities. Practitioners must also be prepared to support varied learning styles, individual as well as group learning, performance-improvement initiatives of all kinds . . . just about whatever they might be called upon to do. The common element, however, will need to be *performance*—the purpose of organizations.

If all players in the corporate world—managers, Training practitioners and workers—can shift their focus so that workers are perceived as adults, the results can revolutionize the Training function. If Training initiatives are planned and executed to meet the needs of adult learners, enterprises can be transformed into high-performance organizations with a sustainable competitive advantage.

14

Training — Better, Faster, Cheaper

[Problems with ISD] *may become apparent as the Total Quality Management approach penetrates training departments. When designers begin to try to meet the quality expectations of their clients, there will inevitably be more pressures to demonstrate the effectiveness of training in the work place, and to do so in the shortest possible time, with the fewest possible errors or failures. Trainers are now being forced into the work place and to use the tools of the work place. Regardless of our theoretical orientation, it will not be long before learning and doing may be inseparable.*

> Walter Dick
> "Enhanced ISD: A Response to
> Changing Environments for
> Learning and Performance"
> *Educational Technology* (1993)

The employer investment in workplace training is estimated at $210 billion annually. Approximately $30 billion — one percent to two percent of payroll — is spent on formal training. The remaining $180 billion — eight to ten percent of payroll — is invested in more informal training on the job. These figures account for only salaries, materials, travel, etc., not for the effects of lost capacity, longer cycle times, reduced productivity, overhead expenses and so on. No telling what the total investment would amount to if these factors were costed out and added in to these totals (Carnevale, 1990).

All told, the employer investment in training is huge. And by many accounts, it is not nearly enough. Aside from that debate, though, the question does need to be raised about whether the current training investment is spent wisely — to accomplish the greatest results.

In other words . . . are current training designs as effective, fast and efficient as they can be?

Upon reviewing their performance in this regard, many Training practitioners will find that they are falling short, and that much of the training in their organizations accomplishes very little. Training designers' concerns about unmotivated participants and limited field support to reinforce employee learning and skill development have resulted in programs that are longer and more lecture-driven than they need to be. Fascination with new technologies has encouraged Training developers to use more-expensive delivery platforms when tried-and-true paper-and-pencil materials would do. Trainer-dependent training designs are subject to wide variations in instruction quality, and the consequent failure to accomplish the objectives for all participants threatens goals and wastes resources. Furthermore, the motivation to increase staff and budgets has led to the roll-out of many training programs that have little impact on the bottom line.

An important point for corporate Training practitioners to consider is that every day they are judged by their ability to (1) add value to their organizations and (2) produce an ROI for the resources they expend. Due to current waste, Training functions lack credibility with management, and the challenge to support employee-performance development goes unmet. Moreover, any waste of resources only reduces what the Training function has to work with to create the impact that management and workers need and expect, and to fulfill its vision for the organization.

Training has the potential to be a superior investment; however, it will achieve this potential only when it has (1) much more positive impact on performance, (2) much faster impact on employees, and (3) much greater efficiency. It is no longer enough for Training practitioners to help people feel better, work better or develop themselves. There is nothing wrong with these outcomes, just as long as training activity also results in performance improvement—the principal measure of successful training.

Furthermore, the corporate crusade for *quality, speed, low cost, flexibility* and *innovation* as competitive strategies demands that today's training activity reflect these features in its design, development and delivery. For most organizations, meeting this goal will require (1) elimination of *unimportant* training programs, and (2) radical redesign of *important* training initiatives.

The Training Redesign Concept

Training Redesign is a systematic process for improving the effect and efficiency of training . . . a proven technique to redesign training for real performance improvement and efficient delivery. It is also an excellent way for Training practitioners to restore management's confidence in training, and to provide more effective support to members of their organization.

The roots of Training Redesign go back more than 16 years to the beginning of my consulting career. I formalized a process that I had developed and used while a VP of Sales for a high-tech conglomerate. I have been using and sharing this process informally ever since.

The Training Redesign concept was first shared publicly with the training community at the ASTD National Conference in Atlanta in May 1993. My goal in sharing this process was to help the corporate Training function engage itself in revitalizing human performance in the workplace.

Why Redesign Training?

One of the questions I am most frequently asked is, "Why should training be redesigned?" Since there are many important reasons, this question is relatively easy to answer:

- *To meet today's new performance standards*
  Today's competitive market environment demands that every function and activity in organizations be as effective and efficient as humanly and technologically possible. Quality (i.e., performance on the job), speed, low cost, flexibility and innovation, in that order, are today's standards for all work, yet most training has been designed without fully considering these imperatives. Consequently, important training programs need to be redesigned to meet these new standards.

- *To create improvements and savings*
  Experience has shown that just about every training program— in-house-developed programs as well as vendor-supplied programs—can be redesigned for meaningful improvements. In addition to significantly increasing the training program's positive impact on participants' job performance, the Training

Redesign process often yields a 50 percent or better reduction in training time and a savings of 50 percent or more of the expense.

- *To restore management's confidence*
Many managers have lost confidence in training as a tool to improve their organizations' performance. Years of over-prescription and under-design have tarnished Training's image, leading management to question Training's ROI . . . not to mention the ROI of specific programs. To restore management's confidence, now more than ever before, it is necessary that training programs be redesigned to add value and generate a substantial ROI.

- *To support organizations of specialists*
Today's organizations are made up of professionals — knowledge and service specialists of every imaginable field — who need to be proficient in their work. These specialists have more complex and challenging roles than ever before, yet less time and money are available to invest in maintaining their competence. The Training Redesign process will help make every training program as effective, fast and efficient as possible.

- *To expand performance capability*
Highly competitive markets and post-industrial technology are forcing organizations to learn new ways to work. Thus many firms must initiate an organization-wide renaissance in self-initiated employee learning[2], development and performance improvement. However, only with effective, fast, efficient, flexible and innovative training can organizations accomplish this transformation.

- *To improve professional competence*
Using the Training Redesign process will also teach Training practitioners how to design new programs that meet today's tougher standards for performance, speed, low cost, flexibility and innovation. Quickly, practitioners will acquire the knowledge, skill and acumen to advance their work to the higher levels of professional competence demanded by more and more organizations.

Meeting Management's Unstated Goals

Training Redesign builds upon the professional knowledge and skills of the Training practitioner, adding concepts and techniques that can yield valuable improvements in training results and efficiencies. These concepts and techniques are particularly important to Training practitioners because, when managers ask for worker training, they have three *often-unstated goals* which Training Redesign can guide Training practitioners in achieving (See **Figures 14.1** and **14.2.**):

- *Improve performance* - the sole reason for requesting training support is to enable workers to perform at a higher level. Having workers learn simply for learning's sake is of no real value to an organization; the goal of workplace training has to be performance, not just learning. Since Instructional Systems Design (ISD) assumes that learning, not performance, is the goal," instructional designers can easily miss the real objective of their work.

- *Do it within the shortest cycle time possible* - the adage "time is money" was never truer than it is today. Speed has become a principal element in offering value to customers, and in establishing competitive advantage in new markets. Training practitioners must share management's requirement for the shortest possible "time to performance" — which may not allow time for thorough design models, multiple-day classroom training and learning by trial and error. Today, employees need training that is "on target, just enough and just in time."

- *Do it with the fewest resources possible* - the essence of economic activity is to invest the least to earn the greatest return. Every resource must contribute value; budgets should not be depleted; unessential resources should be returned. Such economic criteria are essential for any organization that intends to survive or prosper in a competitive environment.

Figure 14.1
Before-and-After Comparison of Redesigned Training

		From (*Instruction Design*)	To (*Performance Design*)
Intervention:	Focus	Individual	System
	Approach	Instruction only	Integrated
Instruction:	Initiative	Dictated	Self-directed
	Budget	Centralized	All levels
	Participants	Top 20%	Entire organization
	Goal	Participation	Performance
	Design	Standardized	Personalized
	Location	Classroom	On the job (structured)
Programs:	Value basis	Pay for training time	Pay for demonstrable results
	Responsibility	Instructor	Participant
	Motivation	Mandatory/entertainment	Strongly felt need to learn
	Class length	Multi-day	2-, 4-, or 8-hour
	Class size	10-30	1-10 or 50-500
	Evaluation	Happy/learn (*Levels 1&2*)	Behavior/performance (*Levels 3&4*)

Figure 14.2
Training Redesign Examples

Company	From (Strategic Obstacle)	To (Performance Advantage)	Payoff
High technology (8,000 employees in North America)	Company-wide 5-day TQM introduction and skills training to require 2 years and investment of $12M and 40,000 days	Redesigned to 1-day class, pre- and post-work, $$ incentives, department goals, media blitz, implemented in 60 days, investment of $2M and 8,000 days	Fast, dramatic, saved $10M and 32,000 days; payback in 30 days
Consumer goods (20,000 employees in U.S.)	Company-wide 1-day strategic realignment briefing to require 1 year, extensive travel by executives and investment of $6M and 20,000 days	Redesigned to 1-hour local briefing, video of execs and workbook with pre- and post-quiz, $$ incentives, department action plan, implemented in 1 week, investment of $700K and 2,500 days	Fast, dramatic, saved $5.3M and 17,500 days; department action plans
Hospital (2,200 employees in one location)	Staff development in 12 critical competencies taught in 2-day class to require 4 years and investment of $6M and 52,800 days	Redesigned to 1-hour class, performance guide, pre- and post-work, performance management; implemented in 1 year, investment of $2.6M and 3,300 days	Fast, dramatic, saved $3.4M and 49,500 days; transformed climate

Figure 14.3
Training Redesign Process

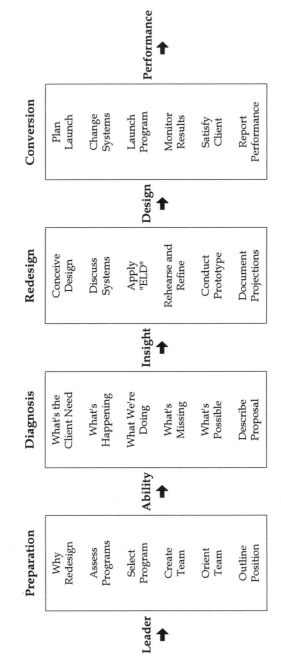

Training Redesign Process

The four-stage Training Redesign process is represented in **Figure 14.3**. Each step flows systematically from the preceding one to guide the effective application of the concepts and methods required to pursue both performance and efficiency objectives. Specific activities are outlined, and deliverables mark the completion of each stage.

This graphic is purposely easy to understand and follow. In fact, one of my goals for this process was for Training practitioners to be able to act with no more instruction than what is provided in the process graphic. We regularly hold two-day public workshops to facilitate Training practitioners through the process, yet I know that some people are able to work from this graphic illustration alone. The Training Redesign workshop—conducted in accordance with adult learning theories—allows us to facilitate participants through the process, using training designs they bring with them. We are also able to support them with relevant technology, and with examples of client-produced work papers and deliverables to clarify activities in the process. Though every situation is different, it is generally helpful to see what others have done. We also stress the parallel project-management issues of content and process: *content* issues relate to the training program itself, whereas *process* issues pertain to the interaction between the people involved in the process. Moreover, we provide each participant with a Learning Guide that serves as a workbook at the workshop, and as a guide later on the job.

Efficient Design Principles

Five design principles underlie the Training Redesign process:

1. *Instructional effectiveness*
   The essence of instructional effectiveness is to provide expert subject matter that is on target, just enough, and just in time to motivated learners.

2. *Shortest cycle time to performance*
   Cycle time is the amount of time (number of days, hours, minutes, or seconds) between the beginning of a training assignment (including pre-course work), and the time when participants are able to meet the performance objectives to

management's satisfaction. Reducing cycle time lowers both direct and overhead expenses, increases productivity, and speeds up the performance advantage.

3. *Lowest total cost*
    The major factors in total cost include the following:

    *   *Participants' time off the job*
        (1) lost capacity
        (2) lost productivity
        (3) direct wage and benefit costs
        (4) overhead costs

    *   *Design, development and redesign costs*
        (5) design staff
        (6) development services
        (7) vendor programs and materials
        (8) subject matter experts (SMEs)

    *   *Equipment and materials costs*
        (9) specialized equipment
        (10) media

    *   *Delivery costs*
        (11) participant travel
        (12) staff and vendor travel
        (13) instructor
        (14) facilities

4. *Flexible delivery options*
    Flexibility in delivery media allows participants to select their preferred media, and makes it easier for managers to maintain operations while improving performance.

5. *Applied science and innovation*
    From performance-support systems to breakthroughs in change management, every low-cost technology should be taken advantage of to increase the efficiency of performance improvement.

ISD

Training Redesign is a logical enhancement to the ISD process, adapting it to satisfy instructional needs in the workplace. Walter Dick, Professor of Instructional Systems, Department of Educational Research, Florida State University, defines ISD as

> *a process for determining what to teach and how to teach it. The assumption is made that there is a target population (somewhere) that should learn something* (1993).

That may be an expensive assumption to make. It parallels the assumption that management made years ago before Deming helped them understand that processes and systems are more often the culprit if there is a problem in the organization. What if "learning" is not the solution? The discussion of "whole systems" in Chapters 2 and 10 strongly suggests that the solution lies elsewhere. The result of this belated insight is that corporations have hundreds of training programs and full agendas with vendors . . . all to meet management objectives that cannot be accomplished with training.

Dick suggests that ISD is a process that is vulnerable to this kind of oversight, and thus in need of enhancements:

> *No one invented ISD. It is simply a collection of processes that were used initially by the military and curriculum developers, and only because there were too many learners and not enough Subject-Matter Experts (SME) to teach what they know. For the immediate future, it may be necessary to add more to ISD in order to have a model that continues to be useful in light of changes in the working environments of corporations:*
>
> o   *Getting to know the real problem - instructional designers need to become performance technologists . . . and get into organizational problem solving.*
>
> o   *Selecting appropriate solutions - we must differentiate learning outcomes in terms of skills that affect the organizational bottom line.*
>
> o   *Using performance support tools. There is a significant change in the nature of the training that is required. Learners will go to the workplace and learn at work.*

> *Just-in-time training is embedded in the work systems*
> *and provided as needed.*

Some people think of the Training Redesign process as another step in the ISD process—a special procedure that modifies ISD for the workplace—to emphasize the need for performance outcomes, speed and efficiency. Adding one more step following the "evaluation" step of the ISD model illustrates the relationship of ISD to the Training Redesign process. However, training programs can be successfully redesigned at any time, immediately after the regular ISD process, or months or years later.

Adding Training Redesign to the ISD process yields three important benefits:

- *Economic objectives* - *performance-improvement* goals and criteria for *learning efficiency* are added, plus appropriate methods to achieve them.

- *An economic-improvement process* - an experience-driven, four-stage process guides the redesign team (or individual) step by step through the required activities.

- *Performance-improving feedback* - full advantage is taken of evaluations and other feedback generated from the original design.

Training Redesign must be a top priority of corporate Training functions. It makes explicit essential economic objectives— performance improvement and learning efficiency—that have been all too casually assumed in the past to be a part of the ISD process. This omission is as responsible as any factor for the Training function being out of alignment with management.

Performance Improvement

In the workplace, the only justification for an investment in training is a consequent improvement in performance. Even bonafide increases in worker competence that never result in improved performance are a waste to the organization. Achieving increases in performance is a complex and challenging task, but it must be the work of Training practitioners. Conducting training programs, receiving high marks from participants, even accomplishing specific learning objectives—all are meaningless and without value in themselves. No doubt such achievements require skill and acumen to attain, and have in the field of instructional technology been the mark of successful practitioners. Not so in business. Performance improvement is the measure of successful training in the workplace.

Several key principles for performance improvement were outlined in the discussion of the Humaneering process algorithm in Part III. These same principles provide a framework for redesigning training for performance improvement:

- *Individuals are responsible for capability* - individuals assume primary responsibility for developing their potential into capability, and therefore must self-direct their learning.

- *Management is responsible for work* - management's real concern for workers begins when they are assigned to work, and is limited to their performance, to their impact on overall productivity and to their potential to create competitive advantage.

- *Performance is improved in whole systems* - achieving performance goals involves many factors that impact task completion, such as job design, empowerment, capabilities, incentives, resources, culture, and so on.

- *Competence is acquired by working* - competence at work is the capacity to perform as needed in a given task or role, and its attainment requires actual or simulated experience at work.

- *Training must "cross the line"* - Training practitioners need to enter the environment where work is performed and share management's dedication to work performance in order to (1) understand management and worker needs, (2) know how to improve work performance, (3) support the organization, and (4) add value.

Learning Efficiency

Achieving learning efficiency is a key objective of Training Redesign. The widely accepted ISD model, by contrast, is a standardized, or bureaucratic, approach to instruction with inherent inefficiencies that increase cycle time, instruction time, and total cost. Because of these deficiencies, ISD is increasingly drawing criticism from many educational technologists, ISD experts, Training practitioners, managers and employees. Overall, they point out the following inefficiencies that are no longer tolerable in today's workplace:

- Training programs that do not improve performance
- Participants that do not need training
- Programs that take longer to achieve results than necessary
- Programs that do not reflect actual workplace practices
- Programs with content unsupported by management or the work environment
- Programs that rely on weak transfer strategies
- Programs that require class attendance
- Programs with unessential content
- Classes longer than absolutely required
- Classes during work hours, unless absolutely required
- Lecture and reading in a class

Though ISD recognizes the need to work within resource constraints and seeks budgets to establish upward limitations, such budgets result in waste, because the natural response is to expand them. In the competitive workplace, the goal must be to use as little of the available resources as possible to accomplish performance objectives. The Training Redesign process identifies inefficiencies and recommends methods for eliminating or reducing them. Because of the characteristic inefficiency in traditional training programs, Training Redesign will reduce training time by 30 percent, 50 percent, or even more. Moreover, 50 percent or more of the expense can be saved, with no compromise in program quality.

Training Redesign—Path to a New Role

Training Redesign focuses Training practitioners on concepts and techniques that can yield valuable improvements in training efficacy.

These same methods can also help lead corporate Training to a new role, in which executives, managers and employees recognize and acknowledge training as a powerful and strategic investment that creates competitive advantage for organizations. It is up to firms to decide what they will do with this potential.

My goal in sharing this concept, as well as the others offered, is to re-employ the corporate Training function to revitalize human performance in the workplace. Corporate Training—with its unique capability to support human learning, employee development and performance improvement—needs to be working on a much larger scale to improve organization-wide learning[2] and support members in meeting their performance-improvement challenges. The time and money saved with the Training Redesign process will help to free resources for this worthy purpose.

15

Internal Consulting

The purpose [of knowledge in the workplace] *is to make people more productive, with fewer job errors, and able to produce a higher quality product for lower cost. The instructional designer will have to move from thinking about "how to train" to "what to change" and how to make the production system more streamlined. Perhaps training should be the last alternative solution to a problem, if it can be solved by changing the production process in a way that makes it more effective.*

> Walter W. Wager
> "Instructional Systems Fundamentals:
> Pressures to Change"
> *Educational Technology* (1993)

Consulting is an exciting profession, whether it is practiced in a large consulting firm, solo, or as an internal consultant. In the 1970s, there were many more *internal consultants* than there are today, due largely to the emergence of unwieldy conglomerates and continuing efforts to improve productivity through time-and-motion analysis. At the same time, there were many fewer *external consultants*—the big accounting firms were only starting their consulting practices at that time.

It may surprise you to know that there never really have been enough consultants to meet industries' needs. As a result, consulting is an easy field to get into, but the fact that there is no systematic way to market consulting services makes it difficult to survive unless you are well connected, well recognized or have a very specialized expertise. As a result, there is considerable turnover among would-be consultants, which lowers the perceived integrity of even successful solo consultants.

Internal consultants and consultants with major firms do not have this problem, but, of course, they have others. Internal consultants have challenges dealing with their clients' perceptions of their credibility and expertise, and with their own perceptions of the risks they must take to confront problems, decisions and authority in their firms. In large consulting firms, the real challenge is just trying to have a life; consultants travel five to six days a week, and take work home on the weekends.

More important, consultants are special people—they bring helpful questions, perspective, insight, knowledge, feedback and *courage* to clients who perceive themselves to have challenges. Note I said nothing about "answers." That was purposeful; consultants who bring answers are often not really very helpful at all. They only confuse people and motivate them to do things for which they are ill prepared. The only answers we can use to make things happen are our own. This principle is based on the stronger understanding and motivation that we have in regard to our own ideas.

Because clients need to develop their own answers, consultants play a role of trying to influence people over whom they have no direct controls. This relationship makes consulting a role that is based as much on the consulting *process* as it is on the consulting *content*. Content, or special "knowledge" (or expertise), is what we typically imagine to be the most important factor in the success of consultants, but in fact content is far less important than consultants' process "skill." Clients often retain consultants the first time based on their perceived content knowledge, but the reason that assignments are successful and that consultants are brought back for additional work is the consultants' process skill.

Consultants find there are *two critical processes* that they need to manage to assure the success of their relationships with clients:

- Establishing a consulting practice
- Consulting for performance improvement

Establishing a Consulting Practice

The process of establishing a consulting practice pertains equally to (1) the creation of a new *organizational unit* and (2) the entry of a *person* into the practice of consulting. Many organizations are now creating organizational units for the purpose of internal consulting for perform-

ance improvement. The way in which this type of unit is designed—
including philosophy, mission, strategy, process, structure, etc. (refer to
Figure 10.3)—will determine its credibility for its consultants and services. Further determining the credibility of its consultants is the way
these consultants view themselves and want others to view them.

Both organizational and personal credibility are central to the
success of a consulting practice. Without credibility, there is no consulting practice—just consultants wondering why no one is interested
in, or even willing to, work with them. A conceptual model of the way
credibility is established and maintained may be helpful:

Conceptualizing + Positioning = Credibility

Concept	*Definition*
Conceptualizing	How you see yourself
Positioning	How you want others to see you
Credibility	You, as an instrument of change

- *Conceptualizing* - clarifying and understanding "who you are"
  and "how you will operate"
    * Who are you?
    * How do you act as a person?
    * How will you operate your practice?
    * Who will your clients be?
    * What kind of relationship will you have with your clients?
    * What are your strengths?
    * In what areas do you need improvement?

- *Positioning* - defining your market and getting the word out
  about your practice
    * What do you do (consulting focus)?
    * What would you like to do (desired impact)?
    * What kind of role model do you need to be?
    * How will you respond to clients?
    * How will you get the word out?
    * How will you position yourself within an organization?

- *Credibility* - ability to elicit the confidence of clients and be be-
  lievable to them. As a successful consultant, you will be able to
  do the following:
    * Know and control yourself.

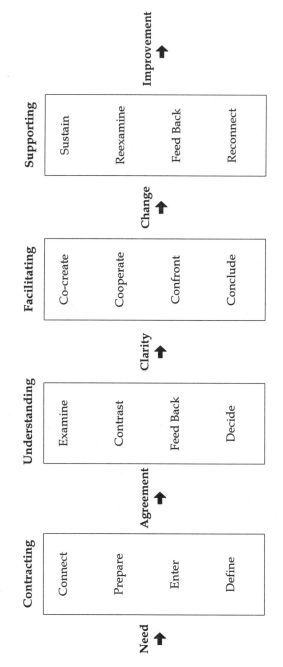

Figure 15.1
The Process
Internal Consulting for Performance Improvement

* Be open to the widest range of perspectives.
* Suspend your need for control.
* Empower others to act.
* Think systematically.
* Know and understand your clients.
* Predict what your clients will do and need.

Internal Consulting for Performance Improvement

The process of consulting is quite simple, but also very complex—that is to say, consulting is straightforward in terms of the principal stages and steps involved, yet because consulting is largely based on the success of a relationship between two or more people, it is infinitely rich in variety.

Several other firms that train internal consultants have models to describe the process as they view it and teach it. Without implying that there is anything wrong or deficient in any other firm's process model, PBP offers a process model that is experience-based, and is practiced by the firm's consultants in addition to being taught in our workshops. The reasons for learning from a process model are many, but the principal one is to assure that every reasonable opportunity exists for a successful consulting experience. The various steps have not been added casually—they are there for an important purpose. The challenge in learning the process is, however, that you can really learn it only by practicing it. Then, as the stages are followed and the steps practiced, it becomes clear why each element is there, how each can help and how you can best perform it.

PBP's process for internal consulting is depicted in graphic form in **Figure 15.1**. The complete description of this process is a book in itself, which is in the planning stages. My hope now is that the information presented here will be a helpful introduction.

Afterword

Paradigm Pioneering

> *To make a difference in the world*
> *and to turn ideas into action,*
> *we must be pioneers in our field,*
> *contributors of knowledge,*
> *creators of solutions, explorers of ideas,*
> *and risk-takers in behalf of society.*

> – Center for Creative Leadership

The purpose of *Future Training* is, in a phrase, to encourage corporate Training and Human Resource Development leaders to step forward and see today's challenges as opportunities to be seized — opportunities to outperform our past.

Joel Barker's video, *Paradigm Pioneers*, provides an inspirational message for Training practitioners:

> *The Paradigm Pioneer makes the vision a reality . . . the individual who, without waiting for the full picture, or all the details, realizes the importance of the opportunity at hand and drives the new paradigm from concept to application.*

According to Barker, *Paradigm Pioneers* share three distinctive characteristics:

- *Intuition* - The ability to make good decisions with incomplete information

- *Courage* - The willingness to move forward in the face of great risk. Courage is the enabling characteristic that allows *Paradigm Pioneers* to act upon their intuition

- *Commitment to the Long Term* - An understanding of how much time it takes to go from a rough concept to a working paradigm, and a willingness to invest their time and resources

Corporate Training practitioners need to rekindle the pioneering spirit in the service of their clients. There have been enough *wake-up calls*, and already there is more than sufficient data to envision a powerful alternative. Now, Training practitioners must trust their intuitive judgments, have the courage to take risks, and commit to the long term for the sake of themselves, their clients and their profession.

References

Andrews, Kenneth R. *The Concept of Corporate Strategy.* 3rd ed. Homewood, IL: Irwin, 1987.

Argyris, Chris. *Reasoning, Learning, and Action.* San Francisco: Jossey-Bass, 1982.

Barney, Jay. "Firm Resources and Sustained Competitive Advantage." *Journal of Management* 17, 1(1991): 99-120.

Brethower, Dale M. "Strategic Improvement of Workplace Competence: Breaking Out of the Incompetence Trap." *Performance Engineering at Work.* Ed. Peter J. Dean. Batavia, IL: International Board of Standards for Training, Performance and Instruction, 1994. 81-106.

Bridges, William. *JobShift: How to Prosper in a Workplace Without Jobs.* Reading, MA: Addison-Wesley, 1994.

Carnevale, Anthony P., Leila J. Gainer, and Janice Villet. *Training In America: The Organization and Strategic Role of Training.* San Francisco, CA: Jossey-Bass, 1990.

Cherns, A. B. "The Principles of Socio-technical Design." *Human Relations* 117 (1976): 783-98.

Cooperrider, David L. Address. Appreciative Inquiry. Dallas, Feb. 1-3, 1995.

Corey, Gerald, and Marianne Schneider. *I Never Knew I Had a Chance.* 1978. Belmont, CA: Brooks/Cole Publishing Company, 1993.

Crozier, Michael. *The Bureaucratic Phenomenon.* Chicago: University of Chicago Press, 1964.

Dick, Walter. "Enhanced ISD: A Response to Changing Environments for Learning and Performance." *Educational Technology* Feb. 1993: 12-16.

Drucker, Peter F. *The Frontiers of Management.* New York: Harper & Row Publishers, 1986.

Drucker, Peter F. *Managing for the Future: The 1990s and Beyond.* New York: Penguin, 1992.

Drucker, Peter F. *Post-Capitalist Society.* New York: HarperCollins, 1993.

Dubois, David D. *Competency-Based Performance Improvement: A Strategy for Organizational Change.* Amherst, MA: HRD Press, 1993.

Egan, Gerard. *Adding Value: A Systematic Guide to Business-Driven Management.* San Francisco: Jossey-Bass, 1993.

Emery, F. E. *The Emergence of a New Paradigm of Work.* Canberra: Center for Continuing Education, Australian National University, 1978.

Fayol, Henri. *General and Industrial Management.* Trans. Constance Storts. London: Pitman Publishing, 1949.

Galagan, Patricia A. "Trends That Will Influence Workplace Learning and Performance in the Next Five Years." *Training & Development* May 1994: Special section.

Gilbert, Thomas F. *Human Competence: Engineering Worthy Performance.* New York: McGraw-Hill, 1978.

Gilbert, Thomas F., and Marilyn B. Gilbert. "Performance Engineering: Making Human Productivity a Science." *Performance Engineering at Work.* Ed. Peter J. Dean. Batavia, IL: International Board of Standards for Training, Performance and Instruction, 1994. 63-76.

Hammer, Michael J., and James Champy. *Reengineering the Corporation: A Manifesto for Business Revolution.* New York: HarperCollins, 1993.

Hanna, D. P. *Designing Organizations for High Performance.* Reading, MA: Addison-Wesley, 1988.

Hansen, Gary S., and Birger Wernerfelt. "Determinants of Firm Performance: The Relative Importance of Economic and Organizational Factors." *Strategic Management Journal* 10(1989): 399-411.

Kanter, Rosabeth M. "The Future of Workplace Learning and Performance." *Training & Development* May 1994: Special section.

Kirkpatrick, Donald L. *Evaluating Training Programs: The Four Levels.* San Francisco: Barrett-Koehler Publishers, 1994.

Knowles, Malcolm, *The Adult Learner: A Neglected Species.* 4th ed. Houston: Gulf Publishing, 1990.

Knowles, Malcolm S. *The Modern Practice of Adult Education: Andragogy Versus Pedagogy.* New York: Association Press, 1980.

Lado, Augustine A., Nancy G. Boyd, and Peter Wright. "A Competency-Based Model of Sustainable Competitive Advantage: Toward a Conceptual Integration," *Journal of Management* 18, 1(1992): 77-91.

Lawler, E. E. *High-Involvement Management: Participative Strategies for Improving Organizational Performance.* San Francisco: Jossey-Bass, 1986.

Lawler, E. E. "The New Plant Revolution." *Organizational Dynamics* 6, 3 (1978): 2-12.

Mann, Charles R. "Education for More Than the Job." *Journal of Adult Education* 1, 1(February 1929): 53-56.

McClelland, D. C. "Testing for Competence Rather Than for Intelligence." *American Psychologist* 28(1973): 1-14.

McGill, Michael E., and John W. Slocum, Jr. *The Smarter Organization: How to Build a Business That Learns and Adapts to Marketplace Needs.* New York: John Wiley & Sons, Inc., 1994.

McGregor, Douglas M. *The Human Side of Enterprise.* New York: McGraw-Hill, 1960.

Mintzberg, Henry, and James Brian Quinn. *The Strategy Process.* Englewood Cliffs, NJ: Prentice Hall, 1992.

Morgan, Gareth. *Images of Organizations.* Newbury Park, CA: SAGE Publications, Inc., 1986.

Nadler, David A., Marc S. Gerstein, and Robert B. Shaw and Associates. *Organizational Architecture: Designs for Changing Organizations.* San Francisco: Jossey-Bass, 1992.

Nagel, Ernest. *The Structure of Science: Problems in the Logic of Scientific Explanation.* 1961. Indianapolis, IN: Hackett Publishing Company, 1979.

Parsons, H. M. "What Happened at Hawthorne?" *Science* 117 (1974): 922-32.

Reich, M. "The Development of the Wage Labor Force." *The Capitalist System.* Eds. R.C. Edwards, M. Reich, and T. Weisskopf. Englewood Cliffs, NJ: Prentice-Hall, 1978. 179-185.

Reich, Robert B. *The Next American Frontier.* New York: Penguin Books, 1983.

Senge, Peter M. *The Fifth Discipline: The Art and Practice of the Learning Organization.* New York: Currency/Doubleday, 1990.

Simon, Herbert A. *Administrative Behavior.* New York: The Free Press, 1976.

Smith, Adam. *An Inquiry into the Nature and Causes of the Wealth of Nations.* 1776. New York: The Modern Library by Random House, Inc., 1994.

Soukhanov, Anne H., ed. *Webster's II New Riverside University Dictionary.* Boston: Houghton Mifflin Company, 1988.

Spencer, Lyle M., and Signe M. Spencer. *Competence at Work: Models for Superior Performance.* New York: John Wiley & Sons, Inc., 1993.

Spitzer, Dean R. "Training Technology: Training for Competence." *Educational Technology* 7(1993): 32-33.

Strahler, Arthur Newell. *Understanding Science; An Introduction to Concepts and Issues.* Buffalo, NY: Prometheus Books, 1992.

Swanson, Richard A. *Analysis for Improving Performance: Tools for Diagnosing Organizations & Documenting Workplace Expertise.* San Francisco: Berrett-Koehler Publishers, Inc., 1994.

Trist, E. L. With J. Eldred and R. Keidel. "A New Approach to Economic Development." *Human Futures* 1(1977): 8-12.

Wager, Walter W. "Instructional Systems Fundamentals: Pressures to Change." *Educational Technology* 2(1993): 8-12.

Weber, Max. *The Theory of Social and Economic Organization.* Trans. A. M. Henderson and Talcott Parsons. New York: Oxford University Press, 1947.

Weisbord, Marvin R. *Productive Workplaces: Organizing and Managing for Dignity, Meaning and Community.* San Francisco: Jossey-Bass Publishers, 1987.

Yankelovich, Daniel. *New Rules: Searching for Self-fulfillment in a World Turned Upside Down.* New York: Random House, 1981.

PEPITONE BERKSHIRE PIAGET

I would like . . .

- ☐ information on the consulting services of Pepitone Berkshire Piaget
- ☐ information on bulk quantity purchases of *Future Training*
- ☐ information on public and in-house *Training Redesign* workshops
- ☐ information on public and in-house Internal Consulting for Performance Improvement workshops
- ☐ information on having Jim Pepitone speak to my group about *Future Training*, *Training Redesign*, performance-improvement consulting or related topics
- ☐ to be added to your mailing list
- ☐ to order _____ additional copies of *Future Training* at $18.50 each, plus $1.50 each for shipping and handling (in Texas, add 8.25% sales tax to sub-total before adding S&H) Total: _____
- ☐ other _____

Name: _____

Title: _____

Company: _____

Address: _____

City/State/Zip: _____

Phone: _____ Fax: _____

Payment Method: ☐ Check ☐ Visa ☐ MasterCard
 ☐ American Express

Account Number: _____

Expiration Date: _____

Signature: _____

Mail to: Pepitone Berkshire Piaget
 P.O. Box 702194
 Dallas, TX 75370

Three easy ways to reach us . . . call toll-free, fax, or mail

Call: 1-800-373-2315   *Fax:* (214) 343-3519